ROADTRIP **NATION**

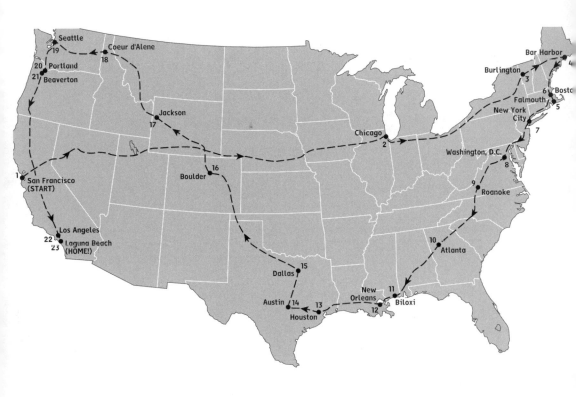

Seattle
19
Coeur d'Alene
18
20 Portland
21 Beaverton

Jackson
17

1 San Francisco
(START)

Boulder 16

Los Angeles
22 Laguna Beach
23 (HOME!)

Chicago
2

Dallas 15

Austin 14 13
Houston

New
Orleans 11
12 Biloxi

Bar Harbor
4
Burlington
3
6 Boston
Falmouth 5
New York
City 7

Washington, D.C.
8
9 Roanoke

10
Atlanta

BALLANTINE BOOKS — NEW YORK

ROADTRIP
NATION:

Find Your Path in Life

Mike Marriner   **Nathan Gebhard**

with Joanne Gordon

Published in the United States by Ballantine Books, an imprint of The Random House Publishing Group, a division of Random House, Inc., New York.

BALLANTINE and colophon are registered trademarks of Random House, Inc.

Originally published in different form in trade paperback in the United States by Ballantine Books, an imprint of The Random House Publishing Group, a division of Random House, Inc., in 2003.

Map by Mapping Specialists, Ltd.

Library of Congress Cataloging-in-Publication Data
Gebhard, Nathan.
     Roadtrip nation : a guide to discovering your path in life / Nathan Gebhard and Mike Marriner with Joanne Gordon.
        p. cm.
     ISBN 0-345-49638-8
     1. Vocational guidance. I. Marriner, Michael. II. Gordon, Joanne. III. Title.

  HF5381.G36 2003
  650.1—dc21

                                                                    2002033044

Printed in the United States of America

www.ballantinebooks.com

9 8 7 6 5 4 3 2 1

THE ROADTRIP NATION MANIFESTO

So, what do you want to do with your life?
"You should be a lawyer, a doctor, an accountant,
a consultant . . . blah, blah, blah."
Everywhere you turn people try to tell you who to be
and what to do with your life.
We call that the noise. Block it. Shed it.
Leave it for the conformists.
As a generation, we need to get back
to focusing on individuality.
Self-construction rather than mass production.
Define your own road in life instead of
traveling down someone else's.
Listen to yourself.
Your road is the Open Road. Find it.
Find the Open Road.

CONTENTS

PROFILES FROM THE MOVEMENT

contents

INTRODUCTION:
The Road Behind the Roadtrip

So, what the heck do you want to do with the rest of your life? We've heard this question hundreds of times from parents, teachers, principals, friends, relatives, career counselors, even the mailman. Not only do they ask that pestering question, but they provide *their* own answers.

"You should be a lawyer, a doctor, an accountant, a teacher. Go to grad school, go to med school. Get your MBA. Go into finance. Investments! Investments are where it's at!" All these might be good ideas, but they weren't ours.

THE NOISE. We call all those misguided opinions "the noise." It's the noise of society trying to push, pull, and tug us—tug you— n every direction. The noise never listens to what you like and what you don't. The noise doesn't care about what you value. The noise just distracts you from building a life that's in tune with what you're passionate about as an individual.

The noise says, "You can't make money playing with model spaceships." Dennis Muren didn't listen to it. Now he has eight

Academy Awards for visual effects, including one for *Star Wars* (page 8).

The noise says, "There's no future dressing up your friends." Arianne Phillips didn't listen to it. She became the head stylist for Madonna and costume designer on films such as *Walk the Line* (page 160).

Fight The Noise. You *can* create roads that you'll be passionate about while also making a living. You don't have to be a prisoner to a job you can't stand. You have the potential to embark on a *life* that you can one day look back on and say, "I was true to myself every step of the way."

How The Heck Do We Know About The Noise? The noise was, and is, after us. We're right there with you. How did we fight it? We took a roadtrip.

Sitting around our college apartment one night, we were hanging out, talking about what we were going to do with our lives. We were frustrated. Graduation loomed and we had no clue about what we *really* wanted out of life.

We sat there wondering why we felt compelled to do the standard post-college things. Those roads didn't even interest us.

One of us (Nathan) was a business major who thought he wanted to become an entrepreneur. Why? "Both of my parents were entrepreneurs, and I was exposed to that path at an early age. But in college I was told that most business majors usually become consultants. However, a consultant's lifestyle—wearing a suit and working for a big firm—was nowhere near what I envisioned for my future. I was more interested in art and design. What was I doing in business?"

Meanwhile, the other one of us (Mike) was all set to walk down the road of medicine. "Most people in my family were in the medical field, so when it came time to pick a major, I chose biology as a logical path to medical school. It was easy to go with the family flow.

One *tiny* problem: I hate hospitals, the lab, and any type of sterile environment. Minor details? Yeah, right. It's only the rest of my life!"

Neither of us liked the roads we were being shoved down. So why did we have to go to work at a consulting firm or in a hospital? After all, these weren't our roads. They were someone else's.

The problem was that we didn't know what else to do. We didn't know what else was out there. All that college, media, and society had exposed us to were the typical career paths of lawyer, doctor, accountant, and consultant. These weren't bad roads; they just didn't fit who we were as individuals.

Roadtrip! It suddenly became clear to us that we needed to get out beyond the borders of campus and California and explore all the options we didn't even know existed. We needed more information. We needed more experience. We needed to meet more people. We needed to hit the road.

If you aren't exposed to a wide range of options for how to live your life, how can you figure out what you want to do?

Growing up in Southern California was great, but it certainly felt like being in a bubble at times. To get outside those boundaries we had taken many roadtrips to all sorts of destinations. Surf trips to the Northwest, adventures in the Tetons, roadtrips down to Mexico. You name it and we were on it. The summer after our junior year we even landed a gig where we got to drive an RV around the country for an online recruiting company.

On those trips, what impacted us the most were the people we met along the way; the author in Boulder, the trail guide in Wyoming, the guy who ran that little restaurant on a desolate beach in Mexico. These were people who lived their lives far away from the bubble of Southern California, and helped us widen our perspective on the world.

While pondering taking off on another one of these trips, Nathan's dad suggested we take a few local business people to lunch and ask them about their own paths from college. But sitting there that night in our apartment, we wondered why we should stay local and only interview business people.

That's when the idea hit us. Why not take a roadtrip across the country and talk to dozens of people who shed this noise and defined their own paths in life? People who were truly happy with the road they chose to live. Maybe they could help us do the same.

Where were they in their early 20s? How did they shed all that noise around them? Did they always know what they wanted to do, or did they have to discover their passion? And if so, *how*?

Building the Trip. Around this time our longtime college friend Brian McAllister was working for his family's business and feeling extremely stifled. Brian was the third generation to do his time at the company, and every day he drove two hours to the office (each way), which gave him plenty of time to reflect on how that path might not be the right one for him.

Another friend, Amanda Gall, had just graduated from UCLA. After five years of playing water polo and having a great time in college, the one thing she had failed to figure out was her next step.

Finding ourselves in very similar situations, the four of us began to build this roadtrip.

The first piece of the puzzle was an obvious one—what would we travel in? We estimated the trip would take more than three months, so a regular car just wouldn't do.

Coincidentally, Brian's parents were donating their family RV to charity for a tax break. Even though it was an old broken down

1985 RV with a huge round nose, we pooled our savings, matched the tax break Brian's parents would have received, and bought the rig for $8,000.

Having spent our collective cash on the RV, the trip itself would have to be financed with credit cards. We filled out applications for several cards, got rejected by a couple, but collected a credit limit of about $20,000.

We knew this was risky but believed that, in comparison to the loans we had amassed from college, it was an important investment for our futures.

Cold Calling. The next step; plan the route and book the interviews. Rather than just rely on random encounters with people on the road, we wanted to research interesting people to meet and schedule conversations with them along our journey.

How did we find people and get the meetings with complete strangers? First, we scoured Web sites and read lots of magazines—*Wired, Sports Illustrated, BusinessWeek*—and if someone intrigued us, tried to meet him or her.

Anyone was fair game; the woman we read about in *Entertainment Weekly* who was the first female director of *Saturday Night Live* (page 68), the chief executive of National Geographic Ventures whose name we found in the masthead of the magazine (page 104), and the guy who founded Clif Bar (page 2). But because we had no connections, booking the interviews was all about cold calling. It took common sense and courage.

We'd look up company phone numbers in the telephone directory, and naively call and try to get people on the phone. If we did make it past the secretary, we politely asked people if we could come by their office and learn how they got to where they are. (It wasn't always that easy, and there's more about how to make successful cold calls in Section Three.) Although many people refused to see us, many actually said yes.

Why would anyone agree to meet with four college kids they didn't even know? Maybe out of sympathy for our dilemma. We would soon learn that even the most successful people could relate to our post-college confusion. To our surprise—and relief—most people had once been at a point in their lives where they had no clue what to do.

We also wanted to connect with students at colleges around the country and invite them to be part of our roadtrip experience, even if only for a day. We had a hunch that students everywhere were feeling just as lost as we were, and would benefit by sitting in on a few of the conversations we had scheduled.

This small idea—parking the RV on college campuses and encouraging students to get out of their own bubble and explore the world with us—proved to be the seeds for a larger movement that blossomed over the next few years.

On The Road. It took us a few days just to get the old RV started and out of the driveway, but once we hit the road there was no looking back.

Within a few weeks we would be trekking east through Iowa, ascending up into Northern Vermont, and then circling back down through the coast of Maine.

Very quickly we launched ourselves into a completely new world that was surprisingly accessible. Without even leaving our own country, we were encountering different subcultures around every corner.

There was something about being out on the road, far away

from our Southern Californian comfort zone, that made us more open to the experiences we were encountering.

A mechanic in Texas or a Lobsterman in Maine impacted us on a much deeper level than we have expected. The social programming we'd grown up with had been banished from the RV, and with every mile we traveled we were shedding that nagging noise more and more.

The range of individuals we met with was eclectic and diverse: a man who started his own brewery in the Northwest (page 142); a cartoonist who got his start delivering mail at the Cartoon Network in Atlanta (page 124); an environmental activist in Washington, D.C. (page 110); a brilliant philharmonic conductor in Boston who, as a young boy, was told he had no talent (page 56); the guy who started Dell Computers out of his college dorm room in Austin, Texas (page 130); a grassroots documentary filmmaker from New York who found success later in life (page 88); and a lobsterman on the coast of Maine who told us that he "wouldn't do anything else if given the choice (page 50)."

It was encouraging to discover that everyone had to deal with the same noise we were experiencing—and contrary to what we had learned growing up, finding your road in life is not about giving in to it.

Finding your road is about *fighting* that noise, and defining your own path based on individuality and passion.

By the end of the trip we had logged more than 15,000 miles, met with more than 80 individuals, and completely redefined our perspectives on life. We learned that we didn't have to conform to fit "acceptable" paths. Rather than being driven by what the noise wanted for our lives, we could define our own roads.

Perhaps we had known this all along, but now we believed it.

Coming Home. For all the inspiration we received on the road, we were hit with an uninspiring dose of the noise, and a bit of reality, when we got home. "*How* are you going to pay your school loans? Time to get a *real* job! Now that the roadtrip is over, what are you *really* going to do with your life?"

The roadtrip had reaffirmed Amanda's passion for becoming a teacher, so when we returned home she enrolled to get her master's degree. But for the rest of us, we still didn't know exactly what to do.

We were, however, struck by some advice from one of the people we met on the road. Randy Komisar, an author and business guru (page 14), told us that even if we didn't know what to do with our lives we should, "engage in what truly motivates you *now*."

Well, what motivated us *was* the roadtrip we had just experienced. Even though that didn't seem like a realistic post-college career path, we decided to slowly engage in it.

Building Roadtrip Nation.

On the road we had filmed our experiences with a few scrappy digital cameras we affectionately named Alberto, Cindy, and Opal. The footage was rough, wobbly, and very unprofessional, but there was a certain authenticity to it that people connected with.

After 3 months, 15,000 miles, and over 80 interviews we had amassed 456 hours of footage. We had no idea what to do with all that tape, but figured that sifting through it was a good place to start. Nathan was able to put his creative and design passion to work by buying a Final Cut Pro editing manual and figuring out what we could do with all that footage.

With no editing experience whatsoever we decided to create a grassroots documentary, and screen it on college campuses across the country—which grew a small but loyal Roadtrip Nation following.

Around this time, a major business magazine wrote a modest article about our cross-country journey to "find our passion." The article led to a publishing deal with Ballantine Books, and the book you're reading right now. We used the funds from that deal to get out of debt, and finish our documentary.

We also began to cold call regional PBS stations to see if they would air our documentary in conjunction with the book launch.

We felt public television was the only network where we could maintain the authenticity of our message, while bringing the road-trip experience to millions of people.

In 2003 this book launched for the first time and our documentary, *The Open Road,* started airing on a handful of PBS stations across the country. We drove awareness of the broadcast through students and educators on local campuses that supported this growing movement.

As awareness started to build, we began working with campus career centers to launch programs, such as Behind the Wheel (see page 195), that empowered students to create their own roadtrips. We believed that Roadtrip Nation could become a broader movement than simply sharing our first trip—it could grow to be a community of students that hit the road and create this experience for themselves.

The first student roadtrip was actually in our original unsound RV—*miraculously* there were no major mechanical problems.

We filmed that student trip in the same grassroots style in which we filmed our first—even using our original cameras, Alberto, Cindy, and Opal. This footage was again edited for broadcast on a handful of PBS Stations.

On our first trip we had interviewed two executives from State Farm Insurance, Chuck Wright and Frank Pignataro, who expressed interest in supporting the growing Roadtrip Nation Movement. State Farm eventually came on board to sponsor the educational programs and documentary series broadcast on public television.

With these new resources, we implemented Behind the Wheel at 20 colleges, bought 3 more RVs, started a "Roadtrip Nation Grant" program that funded independent student trips, and filmed another documentary series for PBS.

It sounds easier than it was—none of us had any sort of experience in building an organization like this, so we had to divide up the responsibilities and try to learn each accordingly.

We aligned our new roles with our individual passions.

Nathan took the lead on all creative film production, Brian with the college movement management, and Mike with the writing projects and partnership development.

By trying to help others figure out their roads in life, we were actually beginning to discover our own.

The Movement. By the end of 2005, awareness was quickly building. Our campus partnerships had expanded to 100 colleges, and more than 200 PBS Stations had picked up our documentary series—much more than anticipated.

Students were taking to the road in Roadtrip Nation Green RVs, or in their own vehicles via Roadtrip Nation Grant, and videotaping their experiences to be shared with people everywhere.

In particular, the documentary series broadcast on public television showed us that "finding your road in life" is not something you do in your 20s and then "click!" you've got it all figured out.

The emails we began to receive from people of all ages demonstrated that finding your road is a life long issue that is pertinent to people in their 30s, 40s, and even older. We discovered that it's not about age at all. It's about having the openness and courage to keep adapting throughout your life so you never veer away from what you believe in the most.

Find The Open Road. After speaking with the 80 individuals we met on our first trip, and hearing about the hundreds of interviews that other student roadtrippers have conducted, the message that resonates time and time again is this:

Find the
open road.

The Open Road is a life built around your *individuality*. It's not rattled by the noise. The Open Road is a path that reflects what is uniquely you.

Do you believe in environmental conservation? Go work in Washington, D.C. and help impact legislation (page 110); Are you passionate about beer? Start your own beer company (page 142); Does sports fire you up? How about working with Michael Jordan to design shoes for Nike (page 148)?

The people we met on our roadtrip all found these open roads. Each identified a passion and built a life around it.

It's easy for this message to get drowned out during times of economic hardship and global uncertainty. When the job market is tight, for example, there can be even more pressure—even more noise—to abandon your passion. But it's during these tough times that this philosophy is most important.

The world doesn't need more zombies. The world needs people who are lit up by what they do; people who can contribute in unique ways that accentuate their distinct talents, passions, and idiosyncrasies. The world needs people who have found The Open Road.

Resist Conformity—Embrace Individuality. As we travel around the country we continue to witness a disturbing tendency toward conformity among our society. Armies of people are marching down paths for no other reason than to satisfy the noise.

Why do people conform? Because we don't know what else is out there. We're perfect examples. The only reason we were going to be a doctor, consultant, or work in the family business was because we didn't know what else to do.

Therein lies the problem. People of all ages are so focused on studying, finding a job, building resumes, and the like, that we often forget to stick our heads up to see what else is out there. We forget to *explore*. To leave that crucial step out of the equation makes it easier to follow the noise.

Explore! The Roadtrip Nation movement is simply one of exploration. We're challenging people to find The Open Road, to expose ourselves to the many different ways we can live our lives before we focus on a so-called career path.

With knowledge comes liberation. By engaging in this search you'll find paths that you never knew existed. One of those might be your open road.

We've discovered that one of the best ways to explore the world is to simply ask others how they got to where they are. Whether it be the person next to you in the coffee shop, an entrepreneur you read about in this book, a political activist you see on the Roadtrip Nation PBS series, listening to others describe how they found their paths in life will help you find yours.

This book is only the beginning of your journey. It's an ignition switch to jump-start your own personal exploration based on what you believe in.

You can't count on school, family, friends, or colleagues to do it for you. Often, they're stuck in their own boxes, blinded by their mistakes, regrets, and fears. You've got to do it yourself. Get out there, explore the world, be your own compass, and forge a road in life that is indicative of only one thing, yourself.

From the road,
Mike (mike@roadtripnation.com)
Nathan (nathan@roadtripnation.com)
Brian (brian@roadtripnation.com)

PROFILES FROM THE ROAD

EPIPHANY ROAD

GARY ERICKSON
Berkeley, California
Founder, Owner, and CEO
Clif Bar
California Polytechnic State University,
San Luis Obispo

GARY ERICKSON'S OPEN ROAD MAP

↓

"Cruises through college" at California Polytech and
gets a business degree.

↓

Works as a mountain guide; travels the world for a year.

↓

Returns home to help launch a bike seat factory;
manages it for ten years.

↓

Begins bike racing professionally; sells Greek pastries
on the side.

↓

Takes his "epiphany ride": a 175-mile one-day bike ride
during which, after five not-so-delicious Power Bars,
he decides to make a tasty alternative.

↓

Founds Clif Bar within the year.

I can't eat another Power Bar.
I can make something **better** than this.

Gary Erickson DIDN'T JUST GRADUATE FROM COLLEGE AND SAY "GEE, I THINK I'LL START A HEALTH BAR COMPANY." LIKE MANY OF THE PEOPLE WE TALKED TO ON OUR ROADTRIP, GARY'S CURRENT PLACE IN LIFE IS NOT THE RESULT OF SOME GRAND PLAN HE PUT IN PLACE AFTER COLLEGE. INSTEAD, IT'S AN UNEXPECTED CULMINATION OF EXPERIENCES AND HOBBIES THAT EACH REFLECTED HIS INTERESTS AT A PARTICULAR TIME IN HIS LIFE. ONE DECISION EVENTUALLY OPENED DOORS TO OTHER OPPORTUNITIES, AND THEN MORE CHOICES. GARY WAS THE FIRST INTERVIEW WE DID ON THE ROADTRIP, AND HE TOLD US HIS STORY FROM THE PASSENGER SEAT OF THE RV. HE HAD A SHAVED HEAD AND WORE RUNNING SHOES, BLACK PANTS,

3

AND A BLACK GOLF SHIRT WITH A WHITE STRIPED COLLAR. "THE ONLY THING BLACK AND WHITE ABOUT MY LIFE IS MY SHIRT," HE SAID. THAT'S AN APT SUMMARY OF HIS ROAD BECAUSE GARY IS DEFINITELY COMFORTABLE LIVING IN THE GRAY ZONE.

I cruised through college not knowing what I was going to do. I was a business major because I always had entrepreneurial ideas, and I thought I'd open up a ski shop or something. But halfway through school I changed my mind and didn't think business was something I'd do after graduation. For a while my life was about music. I played the trumpet, I was into jazz, and thought about being in a band. It looked great, but then I realized that I didn't want to be on the road playing every night, traveling all over the place.

When I graduated from college I worked as a mountain guide and spent a few years taking kids hiking and sleeping outdoors, climbing big walls in the valley or wherever I could go. For a while climbing was my thing.

Then I traveled around the world for a year and my parents were pretty cool about it. They gave me a few hundred bucks and said, "Have a great time," which surprised me because they're pretty conservative. I got a backpack and took off to Europe, the Middle East,

HOW WE BOOKED IT

Mike: I was eating a Clif Bar when I noticed that, on the inside of the wrapper, there was a cool story about how Gary Erickson founded the company. I had an insane urge to hear Gary's tale in person. A friend in San Francisco worked in the public relations firm that did work for Clif Bar, and she hooked us up with someone who worked with Gary.

and India. It was a $10-a-day thing back then, one of those change-your-life-forever kind of trips.

Seeing how the rest of the world lived changed my worldview. When I got home I was kind of down. I wondered, "Now what do I do?" **The trip taught me that nobody has "the answer." There's no roadmap. I had grown up in suburbia with Evangelical parents, and things seemed pretty black and white. But when I came back to the United States, I realized that there is no black and white.** There is a huge gray area, and I was fine with living in the gray.

I went to work for my brother at a foundry he owned that made high-tech metal parts and cool aluminum castings. He had just sold part of his company to another company that made bicycle accessories, and they asked him to open a bike seat factory from the ground up. He asked me if I wanted to come along to sweep the floors or do whatever.

I did that for about eight months, until my brother went back to the foundry and I became the plant manager. I designed bike seats for ten years. Eventually we moved the production to Italy, which was really cool because I got to travel to Italy five times a year. I'd just go there and hang out and ride my bike. I started riding the Alps.

Then it all started to come together.

I had become a sort of consultant for my brother's bike seat factory, making $7,000 to $10,000 a year, living in a garage in Berkeley with my dog, and going to Italy five times a year. I had also started bike racing and two things happened.

First, I got an idea when I was at my mom's house in 1986. She was always inventing recipes, and one day she made a Greek pastry with a meat and vegetable filling. I sat at her kitchen table and said, "Wow! I bet these things would sell." After all, I still had the entrepreneurial bug. I didn't care about the money. I just wanted to do my own thing.

I asked a friend to help me with the business. My mom made a bunch of samples that we put in pink boxes and took around to some delis in the San Francisco Bay area. People actually placed orders and boom [snaps fingers] we were in business, just like that!

FALSE START

Gary Erickson was the very first meeting we had in the fall of 2001, and the first time we filmed an interview. But the day before we were scheduled to be in Berkeley, we were in Amanda's driveway when the RV's engine died! We stayed up almost all night fixing it and left home at 4:00 A.M. the next morning to make the eight-hour trip to Clif Bar's headquarters.

During the ride up, it was mayhem inside the RV. Brian was trying to test the sound, Nate was trying to figure out how to work the camera, and Amanda was on the phone trying to clarify directions to Clif Bar's offices.

We finally pulled into the parking lot where Gary was scheduled to meet us because we planned to film him inside the RV. But right before the interview we realized that we had parked in a spot where the sun would screw up the video's lighting. So we jumped on top of the RV and threw this big blanket over the front window, securing it with duct tape to the roof. It looked hideous, but at least it kept the light out. Gary walked into the RV and had this what-have-I-gotten-myself-into look on his face. We wiped the sweat off our foreheads (the damn air conditioner didn't work), smiled, and got started. Gary was the first of eighty-six people to sign the ceiling. Before we left, he mercifully stocked the RV with hundreds of Clif Bars for the road.

I juggled the baking business with bike racing.

A few years later something happened that I now call "the epiphany ride." I was on a long, 175-mile, one-day bike ride with my friend Jay, and we had six Power Bars with us. After eating five I said, "That's it! I can't eat another one. These things suck!" [Laughs.] We went to a 7-Eleven and bought some powdered doughnuts.

There I was: I owned a bakery, I was racing bikes, and I was in the bike industry. Plus, all the racers were eating Power Bars, which were selling well but lacked taste. I turned to my friend Jay and said, "Man, I can make something better than this."

I had my bakery try to make a product that combined nutrition and taste, and about fourteen months later we introduced Clif Bar.

Was I fearful along the way? I had learned from rock climbing not to be fearful because fear paralyzes you. Years and years of climbing taught me to stay calm, which was key because you can't have fear when running a company, either. Fear spreads.

Last year the company marked the ten-year anniversary of the epiphany ride, and we took employees on the 175-mile trek to celebrate the birth of the idea.

There you have it. It's all been one big adventure.

MAY THE FORCE BE WITH YOU

DENNIS MUREN
San Rafael, California
Senior Visual Effects Supervisor
Industrial Light & Magic
California State University,
Los Angeles
Pasadena City College

DENNIS MUREN'S OPEN ROAD MAP

Enchanted by visual effects as a kid, spends allowance on film.

Takes "practical route" in college with business major; graduates and takes freelance commercial gigs.

Pressure to get practical and make money leads to job hunting; spies "inhalation therapy" in classifieds ads.

In a last-ditch effort to make it in film, drops his price to work on his first "union film," with George Lucas.

Star Wars catapults his career; still working and trying to surprise audiences as well as himself.

Go into something
that no one else is going into.

Sitting before us IN A BLACK AND WHITE HAWAIIAN
SHIRT WAS DENNIS MUREN, THE MAN BEHIND THE VISUAL EFFECTS FOR MOVIES
LIKE E.T., THE EXTRA-TERRESTRIAL, TERMINATOR 2: JUDGMENT DAY, AND
THE STAR WARS FLICKS. HE HAS WON EIGHT ACADEMY AWARDS FOR BEST
ACHIEVEMENT IN VISUAL EFFECTS THROUGHOUT HIS CAREER, WHICH IS
IRONIC WHEN YOU CONSIDER THAT WHEN HE STARTED OUT IN THE 1960S, VI-
SUAL EFFECTS WASN'T EVEN A CAREER! DENNIS HAD NO ROAD TO FOLLOW AND
VERY FEW MENTORS, YET HE CLUNG TO HIS FASCINATION WITH VISUAL EF-
FECTS. WE HAD LUNCH WITH HIM JUST OUTSIDE THE SET OF THE LATEST STAR

Wars film, Episode II: Attack of the Clones. They wouldn't let us on the set, but we snuck a few peeks anyway.

I grew up thirty minutes from Hollywood, but it might as well have been further because I didn't know anyone in the business.

When I was six or seven, I liked visual effects—I don't even know why. There were no video cameras in those days, and I used an eight-millimeter camera in high school and college. I used my allowance to buy film, but back then you shot only two minutes of film, sent it to Kodak to be developed, and couldn't get it back for two weeks! That made everything I shot really important. It made me focus on every little thing. But **it was just a hobby. I never thought it would be a career**.

When I went to college, my folks told me to major in business so I had something to fall back on. I minored in advertising so at least I could do special effects for commercials. **I crammed my classes into Tuesdays and Thursdays so I could make movies Mondays, Wednesdays, and Fridays**.

Between classes some friends and I spent two years making a low-budget film for $3,500. I sold it to a distributor for $6,000

> ## HOW WE BOOKED IT
> Nate: I read about Dennis Muren in _Wired_ magazine, phoned Industrial Light & Magic, and got his voice mail. I left him messages for weeks until the company's public relations rep called me. I had to send a bunch of sample questions to prove we were legitimate. She finally said Dennis was so into the interview that he wanted his son to sit in on it! Unfortunately, he couldn't get his son out of school—at least now he can read about his dad in _Roadtrip Nation_.

or $7,000. He put another $40,000 into it, redid the sound, added some more shots, released it in L.A., and showed it all over the country. I think I learned more doing that film than I would have during four years at film school. So I am really self-taught. I just followed what I liked to do.

My friends and I also went to films that we thought were really neat. Afterward, I'd call up all the people who did the movies' special effects and ask them about their work. These people had never gotten a call from anybody asking them about their work before, so they were thrilled to talk about it.

I sort of goofed off in my early twenties and had, like, four different jobs a year and earned maybe $1,000 for a commercial. I'm an independent person and didn't like the idea of working nine-to-five every day. Besides, if I had been pushed into a job that took fifty hours a week, I wouldn't have been able to learn what I did. People need time to find what they're good at.

Still, I lived at home and knew that I couldn't go on much longer, so one day I went through the Los Angeles Times classified section and found a job for inhalation therapy, something about teaching people to breathe. I'd probably work in a hospital, and I could do it while I continued my hobbies.

Then, Star Wars came along.

Most of the movies being made with special effects back then were union movies, and I didn't care to work on them because they were too structured. But at some point I thought I should at least work on one and see what it was like. I picked Star Wars because I figured that if I was going to do a Hollywood movie, I might as well do it with a director I liked, and I really liked George Lucas. I didn't know him, but I knew John Dykstra, so I contacted him. I pushed for an interview, got it, and told them how much money I wanted. They said they couldn't afford to pay me.

So, literally, I was faced with this choice: Did I want to do Star Wars for less money than I made doing commercials or did I want to do inhalation therapy and wait for another commercial to come along?

I called John Dykstra and dropped my price. I figured it would be a steppingstone.

From the very beginning I tried to separate myself from everyone else. I didn't just deliver a shot, I took it further. I would try to shoot something in a way that people would look and say, "I never knew that was possible." I'm passionate about the end result. I like looking at my work when it's done and saying "Wow!" All the rest of the process is just a way to get to that end result. That's what drives me. The process can be hard—fun at first, but tough to do—and it's really neat when it's all over.

Over the years, technology has made the work easier, and in some ways harder. Now you can buy software and two dozen books about doing visual effects. There are a lot of people coming into the profession that know how to use the tools, but what they need to learn is how to apply the effects within the movie. They have to know how movies are made, about direction, photography, lighting, composition, and how to tell a story. And they must have interpersonal skills, because on every movie you work with dozens of people.

I'm going through an interesting period now because I've

done so much stuff for so long that I have to work hard to make it interesting. So I try to find a hook in every project, something I've never done before. I imagine that my work is obsolete as soon as it's done, so I look for the next thing and always try to come up with something new so I don't repeat myself. The audience can get bored and you have to keep surprising people.

I did luck out. Steven Spielberg and George came along, all the Baby Boomers grew up and wanted to see these movies, and society became very visually oriented. I don't know if I would do the same thing today. I got into this because special effects were just that: special. They were unique and different. They're not special any more. You see them everywhere.

Yet because they were so rare, I went through a difficult period before <u>Star Wars</u>. **I felt like my passion had no future because there were no jobs.** But someone at that time told me, or maybe I overheard it said, that what people should do when they're young is to go into something that nobody else is going into. And if it ever becomes fashionable, then there you are. And that, in fact, is my story.

may the force be with you

YOUR FIRST ROAD IS NOT

RANDY KOMISAR
Portola Valley, California
Virtual CEO
Author, The Monk and the Riddle
Brown University, Harvard Law School

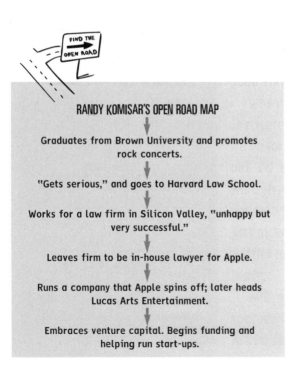

RANDY KOMISAR'S OPEN ROAD MAP

Graduates from Brown University and promotes rock concerts.

"Gets serious," and goes to Harvard Law School.

Works for a law firm in Silicon Valley, "unhappy but very successful."

Leaves firm to be in-house lawyer for Apple.

Runs a company that Apple spins off; later heads Lucas Arts Entertainment.

Embraces venture capital. Begins funding and helping run start-ups.

YOUR LAST

The path is never linear going forward. It's only linear in the rearview mirror.

Sipping coffee FROM THE PASSENGER SEAT IN THE RV, RANDY WAS KIND ENOUGH TO POINT OUT THE CRACK IN OUR WINDSHIELD. FROM THAT POINT FORWARD HE DIDN'T HOLD BACK. RANDY HAD—IN HIS OWN WORDS—SCREWED UP AFTER COLLEGE BY TAKING THE SAFE, PREDICTABLE ROAD: HE BECAME A LAWYER. HIS ROAD OUT OF LAW DID NOT HAPPEN OVERNIGHT.

    AS A "VIRTUAL CEO" IN SILICON VALLEY, RANDY HOPS FROM YOUNG COMPANY TO YOUNG COMPANY, HELPING TO FUND AND RUN THEM. HE'S GOT

Engage in what truly motivates you now. Don't defer it by wearing a suit and going to work on Wall Street in the hope that you'll put away enough money to figure out what you really want to do. You will never get there that way. I can spout off about this because I made this mistake when I graduated from Brown.

I majored in economics, had a minor in psychology, and was in a program to get my master's in economics in four years. That was in 1974 and 1975, after the oil crisis, and I saw economics for what it was. In my mind, markets were about people and how they will react. Using my psychology minor was the best way to predict what was going to happen in the markets, but I needed more exposure, so I dropped out of the master's program in my senior year and, instead, studied computer science and litera-ture and other things. It gave me the broad exposure I wouldn't have had if I had just saturated myself in economics.

After school it was common for people to take off a year or so and travel. It was part of our education. You just got a back-pack and traveled. It was cheap.

I also use travel as a metaphor for stepping out of your everyday experience. That's important. When I was a youngster, I worked as a boiler mechanic, I worked as a baker, I worked as a janitor. I helped dig swimming pools. Today a lot of kids wouldn't think of doing that. If they're going to work in the summer, they're going to work in a law office, they're going to work in an architect's office. They don't get the exposure that helps them understand other circumstances.

When I graduated I did a number of things that I really loved. I helped promote rock concerts, write community development programs, teach economics at a small college. None of these were things that I defined as a career. I didn't think about doing them forever, as the principal thing in my life. They were just gigs. I also took off for four months and traveled.

Then I decided I had to get serious. So I'm in my mid-twenties and I came to the conclusion that I had to go to law school because it would start me on a path that would guide the rest of my life. I had no idea what being a lawyer involved. I had no idea what working in a law firm was. I had no concept. It was just an impression that I had inherited from my parents, society, my friends, and academia.

I went to Harvard Law School and didn't like it from the day I got there. The intellectual engagement was fun, but I didn't connect with the people or enjoy what I

HOW WE BOOKED IT

Randy wasn't lying. He's almost impossible to find. It took us months to track him down after we read his book, The Monk and the Riddle. In the book, he writes about a coffee shop near Stanford University, and we actually hung out there for hours hoping he would stop in. He never did. Eventually we got his email address from someone who used to work with him, and after many months he finally responded to our invitation and agreed to meet us, in front of the very coffee shop that we had staked out months before.

was studying. I got out and practiced law for a few years and I didn't like that either.

There I was on my path, completely unhappy but very successful. I was making good money, I was doing a good job, I was actually distinguishing myself, but I wasn't one iota closer to happiness than when I started law school. And I was miles from the happiness I knew when I graduated from Brown, when I was enaged in so many diverse things.

When you speak to people who have all the trappings of success but are really unhappy, there's a common syndrome: They've crossed a lot of hurdles, but they weren't their own hurdles. They were someone else's hurdles.

It took me a while to penetrate that problem and understand its roots.

I had no affinity or passion for being a lawyer. I needed a lifestyle that dealt more with ideas and creativity. I needed exposure to a broad spectrum of people. I needed more risk. Lawyering is about reducing risk, and I'm a high-risk guy.

My transformation was not immediate. First I stripped away layer after layer of social bias. I had to deal with my fear that, by not being a lawyer, I would lose something that I had gained.

I slowly stripped away my legal life. Next I became a lawyer inside Apple in its early days. Apple was taking risks and trying new things, and I thrived in that atmosphere. Then I moved from being a lawyer to being a businessman in an Apple spin-off. Then I moved to running a few companies. I moved from that to working as a

---

STUDENT FEEDBACK

Lilly, a junior at Stanford University, felt anxious and lost because she hadn't picked a major:

"Randy made me feel so much more relaxed, mostly because he was carefree but not careless."

catalyst for ideas, which is what I do now. I'm involved in a dozen great projects with a variety of people.

I'm passionate about my projects. The diversity of ideas and people keeps me totally motivated. So does fostering creativity. I do it in the context of business because I think business is a really powerful medium for change in society. I use business as my tool, but making money is not always the object. Much of my work is on behalf of nonprofits.

Right now I don't carry a business card. You can't find me. I'm not in an address book. I'm not in a directory. My lifestyle now looks an awful lot like the lifestyle I had when I first graduated Brown. I'm sort of an enigma, and I've never been happier.

Now here's the dirty little secret: You don't need an ultimate goal. A lot of people we celebrate as highly successful didn't have an ultimate goal. So when people look like they have these nicely laid out lives and they look like they have accomplished all this stuff, by and large the reason that it happened is something they figured out in retrospect. It won't happen the way you plan it. It just won't. The path is never linear going forward. It's only linear in the rearview mirror.

TRUE COLORS

BEATRICE SANTICCIOLI
San Francisco, California
Color and Graphic Consultant
Scuola Politecnica of Design, Milan, Italy

BEATRICE SANTICCIOLI'S OPEN ROAD MAP

↓

Grows up in Italy, loves drawing and being independent.

↓

Attends high school for art; studies visual design in Milan.

↓

Works for mentor Bruno Munari, a designer, and slowly gravitates toward color design.

↓

Learns computer design in the United States; returns to Italy to work.

↓

Moves to San Francisco and consults; reputation leads to work with Nike, Apple, Herman Miller, others.

Nothing comes wrapped in a beautiful box in fantastic ribbon. You have to sweat.

As a color and graphic consultant for products, Beatrice Santiccioli has transformed her childhood love of colors into a career. When Apple Computer introduced its new computers in colors like strawberry, tangerine, and blueberry, Beatrice collaborated with Apple's Industrial Design group to create the color palette. We met with Beatrice in her sleek white studio, and at the time she was very pregnant. With her blonde hair, bright red blouse, and thick Italian accent, she made quite an impression. So did her story.

My favorite color is green because it reminds me of the countryside in Italy, where I grew up. I loved to climb trees and play with friends, but it was also important for me to be by myself and draw. That was the moment when I let my pure imagination go and when I'd invent my own stories.

I studied at Catholic school until I was fourteen. I remember the nuns would read us old Greek epics, and while I listened to the stories I'd draw cartoons. Of course they were very upset every time they found me not paying attention. They kept all my drawings but eventually gave them back, and they told my parents to enroll me in art school because I'd be miserable anywhere else. My parents were pretty cool about it.

So I knew since I was a child that I wanted to work in art, but I didn't know if I wanted to be a decorator or an architect or a painter. I just wanted to work with colors and drawings. I generally knew my direction **but it was difficult to find exactly what I wanted to do**. As I started working, I was naturally able to understand what I didn't like. Knowing what you don't like helps you focus on other things, but it takes time and you have to go through different experiences. Nothing comes wrapped in a beautiful box in fantastic ribbon. You have to sweat and be very serious.

I finished high school and moved to Milan, where I started visual design. I also worked as a personal assistant to a designer that my parents knew. I came to consider her my mentor because she really helped me understand what I liked about graphic design.

It is very important to listen to others' experiences when you're looking for the work you want to do and trying to understand yourself. **Listen to others talk about their careers and how they made it. It can give you your first fire, the spark to start you on your own track**. What I remember most about one of the teachers at my school, Bruno Munari, is when he talked about his own personal experience. His story completely captivated me and gave me the strength to try.

In 1983 I came to San Francisco for about six months, when I realized I didn't like print graphics and wanted to get into computer design. I learned how to do computer graphics, and when I returned to Italy I worked at a television network doing graphics for TV shows. Eventually I started working for Swatch, designing watches.

After a few years, I came to the U.S. with hope and my portfolio. I worked for a children's museum and

HOW WE BOOKED IT

Nate: I read an article about Beatrice in Wired magazine and searched for her name on the Internet, which led me to some companies she'd worked with. I called several and eventually got Beatrice's office number. I expected a secretary, but Beatrice answered the phone herself in a thick Italian accent that we'd soon come to know well. I was caught a bit off guard to get her directly, especially since I had no references or connections to tout. So I just launched into our pitch, and in about ten minutes we were chatting about her road.

then collaborated with Esprit, doing graphics and colors for linens. IDEO, one of Nike's design firms, hired me to work on sports eyeglasses, and after that I kept working directly with Nike.

I never tried to look for full-time employment with a client. It's nice to have flexibility because I like to travel, especially to countries where the culture is quite different, to see other ways of dealing with the fundamental things in life. There are always other solutions. You think that maybe the road you took is the best one, but when you see different ways to get there you realize that, perhaps, your road wasn't really the best. There are others.

Sometimes you fail. There are people who can work very hard

but have more difficulty for a variety of reasons. **I'm kind of a romantic person. I think you have to feel involved and passionate about what you're doing.** It's not easy. You have to work very hard. There are moments in your life when you have to work just so you can pay bills, and you have to make compromises. But it's important to fight for something.

EXPOSE YOURSELF

MIKE EGECK
San Leandro, California
President, The North Face
University of Washington

MIKE EGECK'S OPEN ROAD MAP

Graduates college, opts for MBA over being a fireman.

Meets a guy who inspires him to turn down a banking job—"Everybody was in suits"—for a spot at apparel company Union Bay. "It felt right."

Travels world, learns apparel industry; loves to "make stuff."

Joins The North Face to head product development.

Rises through ranks; becomes president.

Do something you have a personal interest in.

The North Face. HAS BEEN MAKING OUTDOOR GEAR

SINCE 1966, AND IN 2000 IT WAS BOUGHT BY VF CORP., AN ENORMOUS AP-
PAREL COMPANY THAT OWNS OTHER BRANDS. MIKE EGECK WAS HIRED THAT
YEAR TO HEAD THE NORTH FACE'S PRODUCT DESIGN AND DEVELOPMENT. HE
HAD TWENTY YEARS OF EXPERIENCE IN THE CLOTHING INDUSTRY, WHICH HE
SORT OF STUMBLED INTO AFTER COLLEGE BUT CAME TO LOVE. WITH HIS TAN,
GOATEE, AND BLACK FLEECE VEST JACKET, HE LOOKED LIKE HE HAD JUST COME
OFF THE SLOPES. HE SIGNED THE ROOF OF THE RV "NEVER STOP EXPLORING,"
WHICH IS HIS ADVICE TO COLLEGE GRADS AND, NOT SO COINCIDENTALLY, IS
ALSO THE NORTH FACE'S MOTTO.

I came from a family of firemen but made a conscious decision not to be a firefighter. It's a great job and after September 11 you can't help but admire firefighters, but it's really dangerous and tough. Actually, my father asked me not to do it. He wanted to make sure I was exposed to other things and looked at other opportunities before I chose firefighting.

That's part of my advice to people graduating college today. **Expose yourself to as many different careers as you can.** You don't have to pick one and stick with it. You can always change. Sooner or later it will come down to your gut. But remember, it's easier to take a flier earlier rather than later in life, when you have a family.

I knew I wanted to go to grad school, so I went right after college. Then, after six years of school I was tired of being poor! Money was probably my biggest motivation to get a job when I finally graduated.

I accepted a job in the training program of a bank. The weekend before I started, I was at a party on the boat of Dick Lentz, a guy who had just started Union Bay sportswear. I'd gone to school with his daughters and he asked me what I was doing after graduation. When he heard that I was working at a bank, he said, "You don't want to do that, come join me." Monday I called the bank and told them I was sorry but I was going to try something else.

It was just a gut feeling. At the bank everyone had been in suits. When I walked into Union Bay there was so much more energy. Pieces of fabric were everywhere and people were making stuff. The bank job would have been standard modus operandi. **My parents, who are very understanding, thought I had flipped out when I didn't take the banking job.** But at some point you just have to follow your gut and what feels right.

Networking is important. So many career decisions are based on who you meet and run into. It's important to know a lot of people. Try to find others whose lifestyle you admire and who seem to enjoy what they do, and investigate why. Learn what people feel so good about. Keep your mind open.

I started working at Union Bay on a Monday, and on Wednesday I was in Hong Kong meeting with fabric buyers and purchasing denim.

A big appeal of Union Bay was the fact that it was a new company run by three guys who had been in the apparel business for years. Those guys were true mentors. They'd sit us down each morning and say, "Okay, this is what you did wrong yesterday and this is what we're go-

HOW WE BOOKED IT

Mike: I got The North Face's main number by calling 411, but to my dismay an operator didn't answer the phone. There was only a recording that told me to enter our party's extension. Well, I didn't really know anyone at the company, so I pressed random numbers—for about twenty minutes. I finally got through to someone in product development named John. He was a super core-adventure guy. I gave him the pitch, we chatted about the waves up in Northern California, and he said he'd personally walk the proposal over to the head of PR. Unfortunately, she was hiking in Peru, so I had to wait a few weeks. Eventually she called me back and penciled in Mike Egeck for our first week on the road.

ing to do today." The majority of the company was just a bunch of kids who didn't know what we were doing.

They gave us freedom to make mistakes, but it became a sizable business pretty quickly, so they didn't let us do anything too wrong. **It was really an ideal situation, like a continuation of school but more fun.**

At The North Face we try to create the same atmosphere. Our average employee is thirty years old. It's a young, very educated workforce, and most are here because they love doing the stuff we make products for. The passion they have for the business is one of the best things we have going for us. At the same time, you have to teach and mentor as you go along.

The best thing about the apparel and equipment business is that we make stuff you can wear. I like that idea, that we make things you can touch, feel, and use.

I encourage people to do something they have a personal interest in. Frankly, the higher up you get in an organization, the more time you spend thinking about work. You never really get away from it. You go home at night and think about it, you go to the gym and think about it. I go skiing and see people wearing North Face clothes, and I ask them what they think about the gear. People are blatantly honest. If they say something like, "You know, this zipper doesn't work," it drives me crazy for the rest of the day. I guess that's an occupational hazard.

I get totally absorbed in the work, and I think people should be. I think people who enjoy their jobs are absorbed by them. If you're not, maybe it's the wrong line of work. **If you don't feel great about your job, it can limit you.** You probably won't aspire to higher positions.

I had friends who were totally programmed, and I admire that. A lot of them are very successful. Some people have a clear vision of what they want, but I think that's pretty rare. I was not like that at all. I was open to opportunities that presented themselves and that is why I ended up on this path. I'm very lucky.

I get totally absorbed in the work, and I think people should be.

BOO!

LUANNE CALVERT
Sunnyvale, California
Queen Bee of Buzz Marketing
Yahoo!
San Francisco State University

LUANNE CALVERT'S OPEN ROAD MAP

Studies hard in college; intent on getting
an advertising job to support herself.

Despite lousy economy lands her ideal job
as a media planner.

Learns the business, works her butt off before
"shaking things up" at Joe Boxer.

Practices "a completely different way of marketing";
wants to start own firm specializing in
"buzz marketing" techniques.

Recruited by Yahoo instead; unique projects
get publicity; gains respect, and a staff of five.

Put yourself in situations that scare you.

After college LUANNE TOOK A VERY TRADITIONAL ROAD: AD-
VERTISING. ABOUT A DECADE INTO HER CAREER SHE MADE AN UNTRADI-
TIONAL TURN. SHE COINED THE TERM FOR A GENRE OF PROMOTION THAT SHE
CALLS "BUZZ MARKETING." IT'S SIMILAR TO PUBLIC RELATIONS IN THAT
IT'S ABOUT GENERATING PUBLICITY AND GETTING PEOPLE TALKING. HER
STORY IS A GREAT REMINDER THAT EVEN THOSE WHO EMBARK ON TRADI-
TIONAL PATHS CAN PAVE THEIR OWN UNIQUE VERSION OF IT DOWN THE ROAD.

I always admire people who studied liberal arts and English—things they really loved—because I was the exact opposite. All I could think of in college was getting a job and how I was going to support myself. Everything I did was about business because I wanted to go into marketing. I was in the advertising club and did advertising internships. In college I sat in the front row of my classes, and I definitely wanted to get all As.

My road was clearly stated because, I guess, I just needed that security. I needed to know that I could support myself without depending on anyone.

When I graduated I knew exactly what position at which ad agency I wanted: assistant media planner at Ketchum Advertising. It had the best training program. But when I graduated in 1985, the cover of Ad Week magazine said the bottom had fallen out of the San Francisco advertising market. It was a little bit scary, but I think that's what motivated me to double my energy. There were jobs out there, and I got the one I wanted at $14,000 a year. I would have taken $10,000.

I worked very hard. Whatever it took to get the job done, I was there. One weekend, I remember, there was a fair in San Francisco and I walked right through it and straight to the office. **I was a little extreme**, yes, but I made time for fun. I don't think any of my friends would argue with that. [Laughs.]

I worked in advertising for about twelve years, and then took a job at an apparel company called Joe Boxer. The company did not believe in advertising. But that was okay with me. At that time I really needed to shake things up and work for a company that had a completely different way of marketing and getting publicity.

At Joe Boxer we did things like shooting underwear into space on a rocket so we could claim we shot an unmanned pair of underwear into outer space. We literally hired a rocket scientist. The media covered it. That's how you help build your brand as a fun brand. My job was about putting a lot of work into insane projects that may or may not have succeeded. **I learned from the CEO, who called himself the chief underpants officer** and the Lord of Balls. Yes, the Lord of Balls.

Why did I take such a crazy job? I wanted to take what Joe Boxer did and marry it to my traditional advertising experience. It was a personal challenge to scare myself and see if I could do it. Sometimes I just try to scare the hell out of myself.

I brought that experience to Yahoo, which <u>really</u> scared the hell out of me. I had actually planned to start my own company called Buzz Marketing, and when I called a former client at Yahoo and said that I wanted Yahoo to be my first client, she suggested I come and work there.

So I did and started this thing. Buzz marketing was something Yahoo had never done before. The company was cautious at first. They set me up with a phone in a dark cube next to the infor-

---

HOW WE BOOKED iT

Nate: We met Luanne through a friend named Phil, who thought she'd be a great interview. She had a great sense of humor and completely understood what we were up to. So we sat down with her a few months after our initial call.

mation systems department. Slowly my projects were successful, and I was given more resources. Today I have five people working for me.

There definitely was a bit of luck. The first project that created some buzz was the world's first Internet taxi service here in San Francisco. For two-and-a-half months we worked with local government and the taxi companies to roll out purple cabs with wireless Internet access for passengers. I remember the night before it launched, I wondered if anyone would write about it. The next morning it was all over the media. At the time, no one was really using wireless services and it was a fun story for people to talk about. It created a buzz. All of a sudden people at Yahoo were like, "Hey, I want some buzz for my department." So I anointed myself the queen bee of buzz marketing.

It's important to put yourself in situations that scare you. As for me, I first built a foundation by doing stuff that was safe

TRAILER TRASHED

AFTER WE LEFT LUANNE AT YAHOO, WE HEADED TO OUR NEXT INTERVIEW WITH OUR STUDENT, ANTHONY, AND TRAILER IN TOW. AS THE RIG SLOWLY ROLLED UP ONE OF SAN FRANCISCO'S STEEP STREETS, A BIKER KNOCKED ON OUR WINDOW AND SAID OUR TRAILER WAS ABOUT TO FALL OFF. A FEW MORE MINUTES AND THE THING WOULD HAVE DETACHED AND ROLLED DOWN THE HILL ON ITS OWN. WE WERE LATE FOR OUR INTERVIEW, SO WE CHAINED THE TRAILER TO A TREE AND ANTHONY HELPED US UNLOAD ALL ITS CONTENTS—MOSTLY FURNITURE AND FOOD—INTO THE RV. WE MADE THE NEXT INTERVIEW, BUT LEFT THE TRAILER ON THE STREET. AS FAR AS WE KNOW, IT'S STILL THERE.

and traditional. That gave me the tools to go off and break the rules and do more innovative work. I think it would be hard to come out of college and, right off the bat, do things differently.

b
o
o
!

A PINCH OF TALENT, A DASH OF RISK— MIX WELL

CHARLIE TROTTER
Chicago, Illinois
Chef
Charlie Trotter's Restaurant
University of Wisconsin

CHARLIE TROTTER'S OPEN ROAD MAP

Leads "reclusive existence" as philosophy and
political science major.

↓

Loves to cook for his roommates.

↓

Reads Ayn Rand's <u>The Fountainhead</u> and other books.
"Things start to gel."

↓

Graduates college, works as a cook for $3.10 an hour.

↓

Embraces the philosophy and techniques of cooking.

↓

Opens own restaurant in Chicago.

There's **no** **excuse** for someone in his early twenties not to pursue a dream.

It costs about $300—YES, THAT'S PER PERSON—TO DINE AT WORLD-FAMOUS CHARLIE TROTTER'S, A FOUR-STAR RESTAURANT IN CHICAGO. HE COOKS FOR CELEBRITIES UPON REQUEST AND HAS PREPARED MEALS FOR MANY PRESIDENTS. THE RESTAURANT TAKES RESERVATIONS MONTHS IN ADVANCE, AND MOST EVENINGS LIMOS LINE UP OUTSIDE. NOT ONLY DID WE GET A FREE MEAL WITH CHARLIE'S STAFF, BUT HE TREATED US TO SOME UNEXPECTED INSIGHTS. A SERIOUS SCHOLAR, HE CAN QUOTE AYN RAND, NIETZSCHE, RUSSIAN WRITER FYODOR DOSTOEVSKY, AND

· ·

In college I felt like I didn't have a single ally. I felt alienated. I really didn't encounter anybody who I could completely relate to. I wasn't interested in the rally du jour on campus or the whole fraternity world. I wasn't better or worse than anyone, I just had a point of view. So I led a fairly reclusive existence. I lived alone, slept in a sleeping bag on the floor, had no TV, no telephone, no nothing. I just read books.

Everyone goes through a point in their late teens and twenties when they question things. My particular metamorphosis happened as an undergraduate at the University of Wisconsin, where I studied philosophy and political science.

Everyone else wanted to use the undergraduate experience as a steppingstone to get into law or business school. Forget that. Undergraduate life is all about finding yourself, reading great books, talking to people, and learning to think critically.

My older cousin slipped me a copy of The Fountainhead by Ayn Rand. To me the book was a celebration of what man can accomplish. I had found someone who looked at the world the same way I did! I read all of Rand's work and then all of Dostoevsky and then all of Henry Miller, then Faulkner—and it just started to gel.

Along the way I began to cook for my roommates. That was the one thing I really looked forward to and loved. I began working in a restaurant, first as a waiter, then as a bartender. I got the bug for the restaurant life because I liked the manual labor. I also liked the idea that you could really connect to another person. Cooking is very personal. I wanted to study that and understand more about it.

I had no agenda when I graduated from college in 1982. I was appalled by the idea of planning a career, but I liked the idea of filling my head with knowledge. Forget the career. My plan was to cook for four or five years and, if I wasn't very good or I didn't like it, I'd have lost nothing. As Bob Dylan said, "When you ain't got nothing, you got nothing to lose."

HOW WE BOOKED IT

Mike: I asked a friend in Chicago if she knew any hip people we should interview in her hometown. She recommended Charlie. I had no connections, so I just dialed Chicago's area code plus 555-1212 and got the restaurant's main number. I left a message with his assistant and diligently followed up for two months until, finally, we booked the visit.

My first day on the job in a kitchen, I got paid $3.10 an hour, minimum wage back then. I thought, "These guys are idiots! They're giving me $3.10 when I should be paying them." I felt blessed. Here I am learning how to work with a knife, to filet fish, and just do this stuff.

It doesn't really matter that you don't understand everything quickly. Dostoevsky says that sometimes it's better to be a little bit dumb, a bit slow, because if we understand things too quickly then we don't know them well enough. Sometimes when we take a little time we gain a more profound knowledge of things.

I gained an understanding of the pleasures of the table.

Every great thing in life practically happens around the table. Whether you are proposing marriage, celebrating a birthday, or the extended family gets together on a Sunday afternoon, it all ends up at the table.

I never worried about what my family thought. **The people who are really close to you are the ones who will not judge you**. People who worry about what others think or say about them hesitate. They may hesitate to make a mistake; worse, they might hesitate to achieve greatness.

Just take a chance. There is no excuse for someone in his early or mid-twenties not to pursue a dream. I think it's about giving yourself over to something blindly. Give yourself in a way that you're willing to jump over the edge of a cliff while not sure what's on the other side. That's how pure your dream has to be.

STUDENT FEEDBACK

Along for the interview that day was Tony, a seminary student at a Chicago college who was studying to become a priest. Despite their different paths, Charlie's road really struck a chord with Tony:

"Just talking to Charlie showed me that if you have a dream and something you want to do, it doesn't matter what other people think of you. You don't have to conform to the social norms of society. It's so refreshing to see someone who just did what he wanted to do."

If it doesn't work, if you don't like it, who cares. You'll have done something that others don't have the courage or the wherewithal to try. And you'll be young enough at twenty-five, twenty-six, or twenty-eight to get on the track for a so-called "mainstream" career. That will still be there. So big deal, you start school five years later than somebody else. But twenty, fifteen years later, it doesn't make any difference.

My career happened as a by-product of my pursuit to learn more about cooking and the philosophy and history of food. **It's nineteen years later and I don't even feel like I've had a job**. I feel a little guilty at times because I do something that I cannot believe I can make a living at. I would gladly do this for a lot less. On the other hand, I could stop and never bat an eyelash. I am willing to walk away and do something else with the same sort of fanaticism. A year from now, this place could be closed.

43

POOF, YOU'RE FIFTY!

GEOFFREY FROST
Libertyville, Illinois
Corporate Vice President
of Worldwide Marketing
Motorola
Accepted at Yale University but never attended

GEOFFREY FROST'S OPEN ROAD MAP

Prep-school kid puts off Yale; bums around Europe
"following bliss."

Needs money, so "talks his way into" copywriting job
at New York ad agency.

Fired up and fearless earns him promotions, then
a new job; puts off Yale for good and thrives working
under advertising guru.

Opens Europe office; lured away by renegade Nike;
"I love to play in the hot zones."

Leaves Nike for job with Motorola.

The best people are not career oriented;
they're just fascinated by what's in front of them.

Geoffrey Frost HAS A LOVE FOR SCIENCE FICTION AND ADVENTURE THAT HELPED HIM FIND THE STRENGTH TO TURN DOWN AN IVY LEAGUE EDUCATION AND INSTEAD TRAVEL TO EUROPE AND THEN HEAD DIRECTLY INTO ADVERTISING. IT'S A BIT IRONIC THAT SOMEONE WHO AT ONE POINT IN HIS LIFE SO DEFIED CONVENTION HAS SPENT SO MUCH TIME WORKING FOR MAJOR CORPORATIONS. MOTOROLA, WHERE HE HEADS GLOBAL MARKETING, IS THE WORLD'S SECOND-LARGEST MAKER OF WIRELESS TELEPHONES. BEFORE THAT HE WAS IN CHARGE OF BRAND COMMUNICATION FOR NIKE. AFTER TALKING WITH GEOFFREY IN OUR RV, IT WAS REASSURING TO KNOW THAT EVEN AN ADVENTUROUS SOUL CAN FIND A HOME IN A LARGE COMPANY.

45

I was the black sheep of my family. I had gone to prep school at Choate and did really well, but after high school I wasn't sure what I wanted to do. Dutifully, I applied to Yale and was accepted, but I decided to take a year off in 1968. There was pressure to go, and people said things like, "You're crazy. What are you doing?" But I was stubborn and defiant, maybe because I'd attended an all-boys school and felt isolated while the world exploded all around me. I wanted to be a part of the world. My parents wouldn't talk to me for a couple of years.

I spent the whole year bumming around Europe and participating in the revolution. It was just the coolest place to be. It was the era of Vietnam and counterculture, and the universities in Europe were being shut down and occupied by students. I ended up at an Italian university with engineering students.

It was an amazing experience. The 1960s were all about Joseph Campbell, following your bliss, going with the flow. I always felt very comfortable with that. I guess I was never really afraid. **I looked at grown-ups and thought they were all a little bit afraid, a little bit tentative. I said to myself, "I'm never going to be like that."**

When I came back from Europe I said, "Gee, I'd like to make some money, because I'm totally out of it." [Laughs.] So I talked my way into a job as a copywriter at an advertising agency. I took a test to see if I was a creative thinker, and I had to write a few cool ads for different products. To my great surprise they hired me. I'd sort of been a little economical with the truth and didn't exactly tell them I was just looking for a summer job rather than a real career.

The most memorable moment in my career happened on the first day at that job. There I was, just a flame, hungry to invent new possibilities. Then I walked into a meeting and had to sit there listening to the most boring, tedious, unenlightened discussion. I thought, "How hard can this be?" [Laughs.] "I can do this."

I could see pretty quickly that the advantage I had over others was that I wasn't afraid. I realized that if I ever got afraid I wouldn't be very good. **The whole trick is to be _in_ it but not _of_ it—to keep a certain distance so you see the whole picture**. That way you can say the unsayable, think the unthinkable, and have fresh vision. I'm not saying I was perfect. There were times in my career that I thought I'd get shot for something I did.

Anyway, by the end of the first summer they had given me two raises. I had an aptitude for making stuff up. Around August I sat down with the Yale admissions guys and said, "Look, I just got into this advertising thing and it's going really well. What if I take another year off before I show up?" The head of admissions thought it was crazy but also that it would make me a richer, more interesting candidate because I'd bring different experiences to Yale.

So I took another year off. The following summer another

poof, you're fifty!

47

48

agency hired me and doubled my salary. I just said to myself, "I don't really think I need to go to Yale." I'd been working with guys who had MBAs, and they all seemed so rigid. Academic training didn't seem to be as expansive as life would be. Even today, at Motorola, I'd much rather have someone who is a passionate, geek-chic, gadget freak evaluate research instead of someone who dictates his email.

I developed a belief that if I got my degree I'd think I knew something, but if I didn't get it I'd know that I knew nothing, and so I'd stay curious and keep trying to make up for it throughout my life. **So I never went to college, and when I was twenty-six they made me a vice president at Grey Advertising**.

I spent fifteen years working for the coolest, toughest, most maniacal guy in the ad business. For him to hire me was, well, big time. He had a sign above his desk that said, **"Learn by being crushed."** The first time I ever took an ad to him he asked, "Who wrote this drivel?" But he was passionate about being perfect.

Eventually I went to London and became regional creative director for another agency and got to do global campaigns. At the time, Europe was much more progressive and all the cool stuff was being done in London. Most Americans were excluded from it, but I was lucky enough to be part of it.

One day the phone rang and it was a recruiter looking for a new head of communications for Nike. I was always a Nike guy. I loved the brand. Phil Knight [Nike's cofounder] wanted to totally reinvent the product and be a company for athletes, not a shoe manufacturer. It shocked me when Phil basically said, "Go

ROADTRIP BATHING

At night we usually slept in the RV in hotel parking lots. But bathing was not something we did in the rig—we used the shower for storage—so we'd sneak into hotel Jacuzzis or pools to wash off. The morning before we met Geoffrey Frost, we hadn't bathed for days and really stunk. We were desperate for a "Jacuzzi bathing session," but there were no hotels near Motorola. There was, however, a women's ministry college. We found a hose behind the school's cafeteria, stripped down to our board shorts, and cleaned ourselves off right before the breakfast bell rang.

tell us what we aren't doing right, fix it, and come back and see me in a couple of months." Phil wanted me to just figure it out, get it done, and show him the results. It was unlike so much of corporate America, where people have to have lots of internal presentations. It was a great experience.

The best people care about only one thing, and that's having an impact. The really great people love to play in the hot zones. There is no doubt in my mind that the running shoe was the icon for the 1980s. It was not just selling shoes, it was nailing the zeitgeist. Today, the hot zone is technology, and I like playing in these types of culture-defining spaces.

The only advice I could give young people is this: "Poof, you're fifty." So, what have you done? Did you have fun? Did you have adventures? Did you do stuff that you really loved? Did you lead a brave life?

MANNY THE LOBSTERMAN

MANNY
Falmouth, Maine
Self-employed Lobsterman
University of Southern Maine

MANNY'S OPEN ROAD MAP

Hates college business classes, works as a diver on the side.

Drops out of college to dive, the money rolls in.

Business sours, begins lobstering full-time.

Questions his path, takes computer courses, and gets a job in insurance.

Misses lobstering and returns to it full-time off the coast of Maine. "I wouldn't do anything else given the choice."

Your parents may not approve,
but go where you think you should go.

Sitting on Manny's WEATHER-BEATEN LOBSTER
BOAT, THE JARVIS BAY II, WE HAD A FEW SHIPYARD BEERS IN THE LATE AF-
TERNOON SUN. WE COULD SEE WHY MANNY'S HIGH SCHOOL FRIEND—NOW AN
EXECUTIVE IN MANHATTAN—CALLED MANNY'S LIFE AS A MAINE LOBSTERMAN
ROMANTIC. HE WAS HUMBLE AND CONTENT. WEARING JEANS, KNEE-HIGH
FISHING BOOTS, AND AN OLD WHITE T-SHIRT, MANNY MADE NO APOLOGIES
FOR DITCHING COLLEGE FOR A LIFE ON THE WATER.

Where was I at eighteen or nineteen? I was just out of high school and trying to pick a direction for my life. I applied to a college about two hours away from home, got accepted, enrolled, and backed out two days before I was supposed to go away. I just had cold feet about doing it. I also had a girlfriend, so I chickened out, stayed home, and went to a local college. It didn't take long until the girlfriend left, though, and I floundered around school, trying to pick a major. Nothing interested me. I tried accounting and I tried economics, but they were boring. I did lobstering a couple days a week to earn spending money.

It was about '91 and the country was in a recession. I met somebody and took him out diving for sea urchins. We split the money and started making $100 a day, five days a week. That was better than what I was going to make when I got out of college.

So I started diving myself rather then taking the guy out, making $200, $300 a day, and then up to $400 and $500. Christmas came and the season really picked up. I started making $700 a day. I mean most people were

HOW WE BOOKED IT

We met Manny serendipitously on the roadtrip. It was actually a weekend that we had scheduled no interviews, so we chose to cruise around the coast of Maine. At a small fishing town called Castine, we met a crew of classic Maine fishermen who took us out on their boat. At the end of the boat ride we spotted Manny hauling in his day's lobster catch and—as we do with almost everyone—we started talking with him. We took his cell phone number so we could contact him next time we were in Maine, which we did a week later.

making $300 a week! College looked like a pretty stupid option at that point. My mother didn't put any pressure on me. She let me choose my own course. **But my father put a lot of pressure on me. I was basically going to live my father's dream, my father's life.**

I dropped out and started diving full-time. I thought the good times would never end. There were so many urchins and so much money to be made. Then other people got into it and my catch started to decrease and the prices went down.

So I went back to lobstering.

It's a primal instinct, hunting and gathering. And I like the freedom, the independence. It's just unbelievable. You don't have to be here every day at eight or nine o'clock in the morning to answer to somebody, or rushin' so you don't have time to stop and get coffee **It's just so laid back.** If you need the day off or the week off, there's no accountability to anybody. The buyers are here. They take 'em if you got 'em, and they don't expect 'em if you don't. You know what I mean?

Once you get a taste of self-employment, it's kind of hard to go back to working for somebody else.

It always seems like there is job uncertainty, especially now, with what's going on in the country. There are a lot of layoffs nationwide, and I'm glad I'm not in that position.

It hasn't all been glorious. You always have thoughts that you should be doing something else. Are you making the right decision with your life? I went to a fisherman retraining program to learn how to work with computers **and for a while I did the nine-to-five, yes sir, no sir, can I have a raise sir.** I worked at a big insurance company in Maine that was trying to upgrade its computer systems. You just worked your forty hours a week and went home. There was no incentive. Your earnings potential was capped. I'm glad I did it but the whole time I wasn't happy. I couldn't wait to get done with it and get back out here.

I never completely gave up lobstering. **It's in my blood**. I can't explain it. Once the sea gets in your veins, it is hard to get rid of it. Maybe impossible. [Laughs.] So that's what I've been doing for the past five years. And I wouldn't do anything else given the choice. I know I'm lucky. Definitely. I am very content and very happy. Am I lying? No, I'm speaking the truth.

SEND THE COMPOSITIONS!

BENJAMIN ZANDER
Boston, Massachusetts
International Conductor;
Founding Conductor, Boston Philharmonic
State Academy, Cologne,
University College, London

BEN ZANDER'S OPEN ROAD MAP

↓

Father sparks young Ben's passion for music.

↓

Submits musical compositions to contest at age nine,
deemed untalented.

↓

Mom submits compositions to famous English composer
who then takes Ben on as a student.

↓

Leaves school at fifteen to travel and study cello
in Europe; abandons the cello when his hands become
too painful to play.

↓

Becomes a conductor, comes to the United States, and
eventually the Boston Philharmonic is founded for him.

A "no" is just a bump in the road, not the end of the road.

Ben Zander HAS CONDUCTED THE BOSTON PHILHARMONIC
SINCE 1979, BUT HE STARTED COMPOSING WHEN HE WAS JUST NINE YEARS
OLD. HE MAY HAVE FOUND HIS PASSION AT A YOUNG AGE—WE SHOULD ALL BE
SO LUCKY—BUT THAT DOESN'T MEAN HIS ROAD WAS WITHOUT STRUGGLE. IN
FACT, HE BELIEVES THAT FAILURE IS NOT ONLY INEVITABLE BUT NECESSARY.
WHEN MOST PEOPLE SEE BEN, HE'S IN A HUGE SYMPHONY HALL WEARING COAT
AND TAILS, BUT WHEN WE MET HIM HE WORE JEANS AND A BROWN BLAZER.
FIRST HE TREATED US TO TEA IN THE KITCHEN OF HIS HOME IN CAMBRIDGE,
MASSACHUSETTS, AND THEN WE SETTLED INTO HIS LIVING ROOM FOR THE OF-

58

FICIAL INTERVIEW. IT WAS A BEAUTIFUL DAY. THE SUN WAS STREAMING IN THROUGH THE WINDOWS, AND BEN'S FACE LIT UP AS HE TALKED ABOUT HIS PAST.

M y father drew me to music. He was a lawyer and a scholar of Middle Eastern affairs, but he was also a very gifted musician. When he sat at the piano and played he was so ecstatic. I would look at him and say, "Whatever he's having, I want that!"

As far as I'm concerned that's the secret: whatever lights someone up and makes him look joyful. I was driven by the realization that music would get me a lot of excitement, thrill, and feedback.

But there were stories along the way, complicated parts. When I was nine I wrote some compositions, as kids do, and my mother submitted them to an arts festival in our village in England. A well-known composer came in from London to judge the contest, and when the time came to give the award he held my composition above his head and said, "These compositions are so bad that not only can't I consider them for the competition, but it goes without saying that this young man should be discouraged from ever composing again."

Isn't that incredible? My mother put the compositions and the man's remarks in an envelope and sent them to the leading composer in England, Benjamin Britten. Four days later the telephone rang and it was Benjamin Britten on the phone! It might as well have been Beethoven, you know! He told my mother not to worry, that the compositions were perfectly nice and if we wanted to come and spend the summer holiday in his village in Suffolk, he would be very happy to work with me. Well, we spent three summers there. He became my mentor and teacher.

Isn't that an amazing story? I love to tell it because when most people are stopped by something, they shrug their shoulders and say, "Oh well, too bad, that's not for me." But a "no" is just a bump in the road, it's not the end of the road. The question should be, "What's next?" What can you do next? Like send the compositions to Benjamin Britten!

There are lots of stories like that in my life. If I think something is worth doing, I'll remove the barriers. **When I was fifteen, I left school completely and went to Florence and Germany to study cello.** I lived in Italy in a pensione with two other students.

My teacher said he wanted me to stay in Florence, so my father asked the headmaster at my school if I could. The headmaster said, "Dr. Zander, how many times do you think your son will get such an invitation?" [Laughs.] My father said, "Not very often," and he let me go.

When my father asked how much the lessons cost, my teacher said, "If I charged you what I thought my lessons were worth you could never pay it!" [Laughs.] He taught me for five years for nothing.

I also traveled around Europe when I should have been in school. It gave me a huge sense of independence, and I got used to talking to people in different languages. I saw a lot of places and felt that I could be anywhere and belong.

I've always had an absolutely clear notion that I could be a teacher, and in that sense my life is about contribution. **I don't measure life by success—not anymore. I measure it by how much opportunity I have to contribute.** And as long as I have that opportunity, I'm going to be a very happy person.

The point is to know what you're after—pleasure or success.

SCRUBS AT THE SYMPHONY

Ben got us tickets to his concert the night before our interview. It was amazing to watch him do his thing, and we loved the show. However, we were definitely the scrubbiest-looking people in the concert hall, and figured that being over seventy, wearing a bow tie, and having a Harvard degree was a prerequisite to get tickets. (Okay, slight exaggeration, but the point is we totally stood out.)

After the concert Ben was schmoozing with people in the audience when he spotted us from across the room and with big, open arms he exclaimed, "The roadtrip guys!" He came over and said how excited he was about the interview. Everyone around us looked perplexed, as if they were asking themselves, "Why in the world is Benjamin Zander talking to those guys?" It was awesome.

Don't look around asking if you're better than the next person. It can't be about that. **Success is really a by-product of something you do. It's a by-product of an effective life.**

Yes, there were moments when I thought about failure. I was a cellist originally, and I developed a condition where I couldn't produce calluses on my fingers. It was very painful to play and I had to stop. It was a crisis point.

When my cello life ended, my mother said I should be a conductor, but I always retorted, "Don't be silly, I couldn't possibly do that." She kept insisting and I kept resisting. When I finally did become a conductor, and a successful one at that, she was no longer around to see it. So after my first CD, The Rite of Spring, came out, I placed a copy on her grave and said, "Thanks, Mom."

I think it's tremendously important to develop a powerful relationship with failure. If you're a coward and stopped by failure, there's no way to develop. Making mistakes is the most valuable training there is. My teacher used to say you can't play great music unless your heart has been broken. So maybe the answer is to have more broken hearts and get on with it. That's why I teach my students to celebrate mistakes. Every time they make mistakes I say, **"How fascinating!"** [Stretches arms up into the air and smiles.]

THE JUICE GUY

TOM FIRST
**Cambridge, Massachusetts
Cofounder and Cochairman
Nantuckel Neclars
Brown University**

TOM FIRST'S OPEN ROAD MAP

Graduates Brown; while "friends went to Wall Street or law school," Tom moves to Nantucket Island.

Starts a "floating store" with friend; fixes engines and cleans boats.

Concocts and begins selling juice that reminds him of a past trip to Spain.

Questions his blue-collar life one cold Christmas Eve: "What am I doing?"

Pulls on self-confidence to overcome fear and skepticism.

Distributes juice locally, nationally; Nantucket Nectars is born.

My parents were like, "Who starts a juice company?"

The small, narrow streets OF HARVARD SQUARE IN CAMBRIDGE, MASSACHUSETTS, ARE NOT EXACTLY RV FRIENDLY. BUT AFTER SOME CAREFUL MANEUVERING, WE FINALLY PULLED UP IN FRONT OF AN OLD FRATERNITY HOUSE, THE UNEXPECTED HEADQUARTERS OF TOM FIRST'S COMPANY. AFTER HIS OWN COLLEGE DAYS, TOM AND HIS BEST FRIEND MOVED TO NANTUCKET—A COZY LITTLE ISLAND NEAR BOSTON—AND STARTED A FLOATING CONVENIENCE STORE, DELIVERING STUFF LIKE NEWSPAPERS AND COFFEE TO PEOPLE ON BOATS IN NANTUCKET HARBOR. THAT SMALL BUSINESS EVENTUALLY EVOLVED INTO NANTUCKET NECTARS, A COMPANY THAT TODAY IS OWNED BY CADBURY SCHWEPPES AND EMPLOYS ABOUT 150 PEOPLE. IT

WASN'T AN EASY JOURNEY FOR TOM. HE WORKED LONG HOURS, HAD TO DEAL WITH SKEPTICAL PARENTS, AND WAS SADDLED WITH HUGE DEBT FOR YEARS.

I've always thought that the period between the ages of twenty and twenty-five is one of the most difficult times in your whole life. Most people are lost. I wasn't even sure that I was allowed to do what I wanted to do.

Right after my senior year, **while my friends went to Wall Street or law school, I moved to Nantucket and started a business** with my friend, Tom. We ran a floating store on the water, doing deliveries, fixing engines, cleaning boats.

We eventually got our commercial fisherman licenses and ran a scallop shanty. Fishermen would come to us to weigh their scallops, then we'd buy them and ship them to Boston. It was heaven on earth. We worked from 4:30 A.M. until 9:00 at night. I'd fall asleep, wake up, and couldn't wait to get to work in the morning. It was interesting and challenging. I mean, our friends in Nantucket were drinking and partying, but we didn't even want to.

I wore these big rubber boots and the whole fishing outfit. I'm sure my parents looked at me and said, "What is this kid doing?" After all, at Brown I had started in pre-med!

Yes, I felt pressure from my parents. I grew up in a pretty conservative town and there were certain expectations. My parents were willing to let me find my way, but I think my mother was hoping I'd be a lawyer because she thought I'd be good at it. At one point, she had also wanted me to be a doctor.

Still, I questioned myself.

I clearly remember one night. It was Christmas Eve and my friends had gone home to be with their families. It was the end of the workday, the temperature had dropped from about 45 to 10 degrees in just a few hours, and I had to wash the shells and scallop guts out of the buckets. I went to the beach to dump the scallops off the dock. I was alone, spraying out these buckets. The water was turning to ice under my feet, but I didn't even notice it. Suddenly, my feet slipped out from under me, I slammed onto the dock, and the hose started spraying water everywhere!

So there I am, just lying on the dock on a perfectly clear night, staring up at the sky and I thought to myself, "**WHAT THE HELL AM I DOING?** I'm washing out scallop guts from buckets in Nantucket on Christmas Eve! I'm twenty-three years old, I went to Brown, my parents are pissed at me, I should be doing something different."

How did I overcome all the skepticism? Ironically, I felt that I was capable of pulling off anything because ever since I was a little kid my parents had told me that I could do things. They didn't tell me I was the greatest kid in the world, but they told me I was bright and capable of doing whatever I wanted.

HOW WE BOOKED IT

We had known about "the juice guys," as Tom and Tom call themselves, for a while and were big fans. We called 411 in Boston and asked for the number of Nantucket Nectars headquarters. We phoned and asked the operator for "the Toms," and she sent us directly to the public relations department. We left a message for the PR rep Amy, but she didn't call back. We left message after message for several weeks. When she finally did call us back, she was super nice. She had been so busy she couldn't get to us right away, but she was pumped about our project. We hit it off, and she set up the meeting with Tom First.

So I ended up staying on Nantucket and looking for a way to create a year-round business. I had been in Spain during my senior year and tasted this juice. I always liked to cook, so we started making juice and selling it off the boat. My parents were like, "Who starts a juice company?" I used to go home and bring bottles with hand-drawn labels on them, and my parents just thought it was cute.

Soon we started selling the juice through stores. We hired a bunch of friends who drove around in a van delivering it. Then we brought it off the island to Cape Cod and Martha's Vineyard, then to Washington D.C., New York, and Philadelphia. We started mass producing it. All of a sudden it was a company! Two years after we started, my mother heard me on the radio doing a commercial and was like, "Oh my god, my son really does have a business."

We almost went out of business fifteen times. I lived for six years with huge debt from trying to build this company, and I borrowed money from friends, parents, and others. Eventually I paid it all off and started making money.

I used to ask myself, "What am I contributing to the world by making juice? You can knock lawyers and you can knock doctors, but at least people need them. So, why am I making juice?"

Ultimately, my sense was that Tom and I had pulled together a group of employees who loved trying to make a great product and getting it into people's hands. Plus, we all loved coming to the office every day and enjoyed working together. Building a place where people like to come is a great gift to give. I think that's a great contribution, and I'm proud of it.

No one could have predicted my path. It took me many years to figure out what the

heck I was doing. And that's true for a lot of people. One place just gets you to the next.

It's like hiking. You get to a spot and see a vista that you never even knew existed. And then you come to another place and see another unexpected view. Out of college you're right at the base of the hill. You wonder what the hike will be like, which path you should take. But there are a million different paths and many of them connect. They're not mutually exclusive. Whatever path you take leads to another, unexpected view of life. After twelve years out of college, I feel like I have just gotten to another place and all of a sudden I can see things that I never saw before.

YES, YOU CAN GET PAID TO DO THE FUN STUFF

BETH McCARTHY MILLER

New York, New York
Director, Saturday Night Live and
MTV Video Music Awards
NBC
University of Maryland

BETH McCARTHY MILLER'S OPEN ROAD MAP

↓

Works at college radio and TV stations.

↓

Interns at CNN and realizes she "didn't have the stomach" for hard news.

↓

Gets $150-a-week assistant gig at MTV in network's early days. Works at Gap for extra money.

↓

Learns production, works hard, gets to direct new shows like Unplugged.

↓

Directs The Jon Stewart Show until it's cancelled.

↓

Recommended for—and gets—job as Saturday Night Live director.

Don't completely abandon your **passion** just because you won't make money or get a job right away.

$\mathcal{W}e\ met\ \mathcal{B}eth$ ABOUT A MONTH AFTER THE TERRORIST AT-
TACKS ON SEPTEMBER 11, 2001, AND JUST DAYS AFTER ANTHRAX HAD BEEN
FOUND IN NBC'S NEWSROOMS AT ROCKEFELLER CENTER IN MANHATTAN. STILL,
BETH WAS IN GOOD SPIRITS WHEN SHE TALKED WITH US IN THE WRITERS'
CONFERENCE ROOM. IT WAS VERY COOL BEING THERE, SURROUNDED BY PHO-
TOS FROM FAMOUS SATURDAY NIGHT LIVE SKITS AND JUST DOWN THE HALL
FROM THE STUDIO. SHE'S REALLY WITTY AND SPEAKS WITH A LAID-BACK,
RASPY VOICE. ACTUALLY, BETH SEEMED MORE LIKE A BUDDY WE'D GRAB A
BEER WITH THAN A BIG-TIME TELEVISION DIRECTOR.

Do you know how few people like what they do for a living? I've had so many people look at me and say, "You don't know how lucky you are that at nineteen you knew exactly what you wanted to do." But all I knew was that I wanted to do something in entertainment. I didn't know what. Believe me, it was not like I was eighteen and went, "Okay, I'm going to be directing Saturday Night Live." I just knew I wanted to be in the industry.

I was a total music kid. I would sit in my room and listen to music all day. My dad loved big-band music. My mom took us to Broadway shows and I liked Motown, the Beatles. I also loved TV, but we didn't get to watch it a lot. We had to ask permission, so it was always a treat.

In high school, whenever the class put together a project for an assembly, I wrote it with my best friend and everyone else performed it. I was the big bossy one who put it together [laughs]. I loved being part of the creative process, but I was very self-conscious. I didn't want to be an actress, because I don't really like being in front of a camera at all.

I went to the University of Maryland in 1981 and got a B.A. in radio, television, and film with a double major in government and politics. My dad sometimes made jokes that I was a communications major. I figured I'd go into hard news after college because I didn't think I could get paid to do fun stuff.

I worked at the college FM and AM radio stations and the TV stations. **I learned more in a day at the radio station than I did reading about it over a se-**

mester in a book. When you have hands-on experience, when you are physically in the world, you learn so much more. It adds another layer to your understanding. So I took advantage of those opportunities.

At college we had a pretty good career department. I got an internship at CNN's Washington bureau, where I did everything. I ran the prompter, I did camera, I ran cable. When I was only twenty, I cut packages that aired. It was an unbelievable experience.

By the time I got out, I hated news. **I didn't have the stomach for it**. It was hard for me that the most exciting days at CNN were when something horrible happened. I don't have the capacity to handle that, and I didn't enjoy it. There was just no way that I could be a person who sticks a camera in somebody's face after they just lost a family member and asks, "So, how do you feel?" It's great that people can do it. I just can't.

Were my parents upset? Well, my dad died when I was a freshman in college, so he never knew. I don't think my mom was shocked. She knew that news wasn't what I thought it was going to be. So when I graduated I came home. I'm the last of

HOW WE BOOKED IT

Mike: I first read about Beth in Entertainment Weekly magazine at a newsstand right near my house. I dialed 212-555-1212 and asked for the general information number for Saturday Night Live. I got the main number for NBC and was transferred to SNL's operator. I explained our project to the man who answered the phone and, luckily, his situation was similar to mine: He was also trying to figure out his future. He gave me Beth's direct phone line, and every week for the next seven weeks I left her an enthusiastic message. Finally, Beth called my cell phone! She actually thanked me for being so persistent and said she'd been swamped directing the MTV Video Music Awards. We booked a date with Beth two months ahead.

nine kids, and one of my brothers was doing legal work for MTV and told me about its internship program. I think you got paid like $150 a week. I got the internship and went there in the summer of 1985, working in the acquisitions department.

I had the best timing in the world. Back then MTV was not a full production company. It basically did its own video jockey (VJ) segments but bought all the other shows. So I worked in the department that bought the programs. I worked my butt off.

THE RV MEETS NYC

The day we arrived in New York was only one month after the September 11 terrorist attacks and the city was on high alert. First, we had to get the RV past the police who were inspecting every vehicle that drove over any bridge into the city. The cops actually came into the RV to check it out. Eventually they realized we were harmless and let us go. Once we made it into Manhattan, we tried our best to maneuver the forty-foot beast through the city's con-

fusing grid of one-way streets. Parking the RV at Rockefeller Center was another challenge. No Parking signs and police were everywhere, and there was no way we could fit the RV in an underground garage. We left it parked with Amanda on 55th Street and hoped she would still be there when we got back. Luckily, she was.

At the end of August a job became available so I finished my internship and the talent department hired me to work on the <u>Video Music Awards</u>. It was the year they were giving Bob Geldof a special award for Live Aid, and my job was to take care of him and his family while they were in New York, which was great.

Then a job opened up in the studio and I started working there, making like $14,000 a year as a line producer's assistant. I worked with the talent department a lot and thought, "Oh, I want to do that for a living." But I would have been terrible at it! It takes a certain personality to check people's plane flights and make sure they have fruit baskets in their rooms.

I'd also fill in and be a production assistant when somebody called in sick. Instead of trying to find a P.A. for the day, they'd have me do it.

I trained as an associate director and associate producer. I was twenty-four, making no money, and waiting tables on weekends so I could live in Hoboken, New Jersey. **At that point I was not making career choices. I just made decisions based on whether or not I'd have to work at the Gap during Christmas.** I'd take a job if it meant another $5,000 a year. I'm a very practical person, and parts of my decisions early on were based on whether I could make more money. That was just being realistic.

My mom saw how happy I was. I think when your parents see you working all week and commuting to New York to work a job where you're making only $14,000 a year, they understand you have a passion for it.

While there is luck involved, there's also hard work in anything that you do. Remember, I was working a lot of hours and making no money. Some people just skate through. There are people who get promotions who shouldn't, but they eventually get found out. And I honestly feel that if you work hard, if you have a passion for what you do, people will recognize it eventually.

There were two directors at MTV who really supported me. I was about to take a full-time job as a producer when the director that I worked with sat me down and said that I really should direct. At that point I didn't even know I wanted to be a director. He said a job would open in six months and that I should hang tight. I stuck it out and started directing when I was twenty-five at MTV. I was very young for the job.

MTV had a sink-or-swim mentality. They gave opportunities to people who stepped up to the plate. I got really lucky because I was there when MTV started making its own programming in 1986 and 1987. They'd come to me and say, "You know how to do a game show?" No. "Well, figure it out." I got tons of experience doing all kinds of programming. I did the pilot for Unplugged. I worked on Remote Control as an assistant director. I did The Week in Rock, The Ben Stiller Show, the New Year's Eve special and many big concerts. I was the luckiest girl in the world!

I'll never forget when this woman from the development department at MTV came to me and said, "You know I'm doing a pilot for Jon Stewart and I don't really have any money. I'm bringing in producers but I can't afford a director. Will you do this for me?" I said absolutely, not a problem. I had met Jon and knew he was a star. Smart. Intelligent. Funny. I left MTV to work with him.

The week The Jon Stewart Show got cancelled, I got a call

from both Letterman and <u>Saturday Night Live</u>. I mean I hadn't even started looking for a job yet! I just lucked out. The guy who was directing <u>SNL</u> for like a billion years was retiring and they were looking for someone. One of the set designers who did a bunch of MTV sets for me told Lorne Michaels, the show's producer, that he knew someone who just lost her job, and I got the call. How lucky is that! I obviously had a positive experience with the guy who recommended me, but it was very lucky that both those shows were looking for a director at the time.

When you come to work here, you are definitely a wrench thrown into a very well-oiled machine. The first six months I was terrified and such a deer in the headlights that I didn't even understand the experience. Then one day I was standing in the hallway and looking at pictures with all the classic sketches on the wall and I thought, "Oh my god, I work at <u>Saturday Night Live</u>."

The biggest piece of advice I would give anybody graduating college right now is to work hard. Do not completely abandon your passion just because you won't make money or get a job right away. Realize there might be some sacrifices, but if you persevere you'll be successful at whatever you do. Not every experience is, "wow, I am so glad I'm doing this." But it might open up the doors for something else.

NICHE PHOTOGRAPHY

TIMOTHY GREENFIELD-SANDERS
New York, New York
Celebrity Portrait Photographer/Filmmaker
Columbia University;
American Film Institute

TIMOTHY GREENFIELD-SANDERS'S OPEN ROAD MAP

Guidance counselor dissuades him from film school,
majors in art history instead. "He was right."

Graduates from Columbia; gets job as shoe salesman,
then off to American Film Institute in California.

Volunteers to photograph school's speakers—
actors, directors—who teach him.

So happy taking pictures that he "didn't really
think about a career."

Buys old, large-format camera, returns to New York,
and photographs people in art world.

"Pays dues"; befriends struggling artists
who rise to fame like he did.

Full circle: Returns to film; produces,
directs documentary about Lou Reed; wins Grammy.

Build your own **network** in the field that interests you.

Timothy Greenfield-Sanders BUILT HIS
CAREER PHOTOGRAPHING PEOPLE ASSOCIATED WITH THE ART WORLD—
ARTISTS, CRITICS, ART COLLECTORS, AND WRITERS. HIS WORK HANGS IN MU-
SEUMS, GRACES THE COVERS OF NATIONAL MAGAZINES LIKE GQ AND TIME, AND
IS FEATURED IN TWO BOOKS. WE VISITED TIMOTHY IN MANHATTAN'S EAST
VILLAGE, IN A BEAUTIFUL BUILDING THAT SERVES AS HIS HOME AND STUDIO,
AND IS DECORATED WITH ORIGINAL PAINTINGS BY THE LIKES OF ANDY WARHOL
AND JASPER JOHNS. WE CONDUCTED THE INTERVIEW IN TIMOTHY'S STUDIO AND
GOT TO WATCH HIM DO A SHOOT. NO, HE DIDN'T TAKE OUR PICTURE, BUT WE
TOOK HIS.

In high school I wanted to be a filmmaker, but my guidance counselor wouldn't let me go to film school. He said I was too smart and should get a prestigious degree from a good school. He was right. Without my degree in art history from Columbia University, I wouldn't have a sense of famous paintings or how to compose people for a shot. I wouldn't know many things.

But I still pursued filmmaking and was able to convince teachers that I could make films for their courses instead of writing thesis papers. For about six months after Columbia, I sold dance shoes at a store called Capezio and projected films at night. That's how I made money. I was a very good salesman. [Smiles.]

When I got into the American Film Institute at age twenty-three, I thought I'd go for six months and if it didn't work out I'd leave. Karin [his wife] and I were living together at the time, and she got into law school in California, so we just picked up and went. We weren't committed to California. If we hated it, we'd leave.

AFI needed someone to take photographs of visiting speakers, like Alfred Hitchcock and Henry Fonda, but

HOW WE BOOKED IT

Nate: A year before we interviewed Timothy, we actually met him at the opening night of Annette Lemieux's art exhibition in New York. He was walking around with a video camera and, being curious, we asked him what kind of work he did. In turn we filled him in about the roadtrip project. He thought it was cool and gave us one of his funky business cards. A few months later I emailed him but screwed up and began the note, "Hey, Tom." His return email corrected me, and I felt like an idiot. Luckily it didn't hurt us, and as the date of our return visit to New York got closer, we nailed down a time to stop by his home and studio.

no one would do it. I volunteered and was able to spend time with people I photographed. They literally taught me. **Bette Davis once said to me, "Bring your fucking camera up here—don't shoot from below. Don't you know that?"** That's how I learned, and when school ended I had my degree and an amazing portfolio of Hollywood legends. I was just twenty-five.

I knew I would be a photographer because I liked it more than anything else. Hollywood filmmaking was so collaborative and, to me, it wasn't an art form. It was more like factory work, unless you were the director or the producer. But as a photographer I was the artist and it was my picture. It was crappy, or it was great, but either way it was mine. Back in those days I was so happy taking pictures that I didn't really think about having some great career.

Before we left Hollywood I changed from using a 35 mm camera to a giant, 11-inch-by-14-inch view camera. I fell in love with it. It made me rethink the way I took pictures because I could only shoot two to three frames. It's not like shooting thirty-six pictures on a roll of film and hoping you get a good one. You have to think about every little bit. It's a whole different world. Plus, practically no one was shooting large format in the 1970s. I'd found an unfashionable area.

So I came back to New York and worked as a photographer. **I don't think I had a plan—things just sort of happened.** Maybe I made them happen because consciously or unconsciously I moved in certain directions.

I began by photographing people I knew, and through my father-in-law the people I knew were abstract expressionist painters, like Willem deKooning and Larry Rivers. All these people agreed to pose for me. I shot young artists who weren't very famous and other people who no one else was photographing.

It was luck that I started exhibiting. I met someone who introduced me to a dealer who liked my work, so I ended up having a show of artists from the 1950s, and everything snowballed from there.

After my first show of abstract expressionist artists, I moved on to photographing art critics. Critics were an untouched subject, and that appealed to me. I did forty portraits, and it was a great show because everyone wanted to see what these people looked like. From there I started thinking about my work as a series.

I got into fashion because the woman who ran a Japanese fashion house saw my work in a museum in Japan and asked if I would shoot people in the art world wearing her clothes. Those pictures became widely known and I started to shoot fashion. But I don't think of myself as a fashion photographer. I'm a portrait photographer. I'm good with people and I love shooting them. I'm not interested in still lifes or landscapes, like Ansel Adams. I'd be bored out of my mind waiting for the light to change.

I've been very lucky because **I've followed what I wanted to do from the beginning,** and I was able to support myself. That's one way photography is different from painting: You can more easily support yourself using your talent. I also do print ads and editorial work.

The art world is very small, very trendy, very political, and very complicated. So much is about meeting people and building your own network in a field that you're interested in. I started out working with assistants to assistant photo editors. They were kids back then and now they're the photo editors of major magazines. That's how I get a lot of big celebrity portraits. They commission me to do, say, a magazine shot of Hillary Clinton. I've become known as someone who is good, precise, and can work quickly. **I had fourteen minutes to shoot Colin Powell for the cover of _Time_**.

The best way for young artists to get out there is to work for established artists. You can have more success if someone tells a dealer they love your work than by walking into a gallery yourself. Just being in a studio is a great way to meet other young artists and dealers. It opens all kinds of doors and gets you connections, even just by answering phones. That's how the art world works. Many of the assistants who have worked for me have gone on to have tremendous success. Whatever you do, you have to pay your dues.

PEACE, LOVE, AND BOOKS

LEONARD RIGGIO
New York, New York
Founder and Chairman
Barnes & Noble Inc.
New York University,
Never Graduated

FIND THE OPEN ROAD

LEN RIGGIO'S OPEN ROAD MAP

↓

Grows up happy with few expectations in "provincial," post–World War II Brooklyn.

↓

Works in college bookstore while studying engineering.

↓

Store introduces him to other cultures, ideas; engineering loses appeal.

↓

Antsy to improve store but can't; opens full-service student bookstore.

↓

"Hustles like crazy"; calculates growth; feels obliged to take opportunities as they arise.

↓

Hands presidency to brother; still chairman; now exploring "knowledge for its own sake."

I never did it to make tons of money.
That was never the dream.

𝓛𝓮𝓷 𝓡𝓲𝓰𝓰𝓲𝓸 OPENED HIS FIRST BOOKSTORE IN 1965, AND SIX YEARS LATER BOUGHT A STORE NAMED BARNES & NOBLE. WE WERE RUNNING LATE FOR OUR MEETING WITH LEN BUT, MIRACULOUSLY, FOUND A FIVE-CAR PARKING SPOT FOR THE RV JUST DOWN THE STREET FROM BARNES & NOBLE'S MANHATTAN HEADQUARTERS. WHEN WE FINALLY SPOKE WITH HIM, HE SERVED US CAPPUCCINOS AND HOT COCOA IN TALL GLASSES. AT THE TIME HE WAS CHIEF EXECUTIVE OFFICER OF THE COMPANY, BUT A FEW MONTHS LATER, IN FEBRUARY 2002, HIS BROTHER STEPHEN BECAME CEO. LEN REMAINS CHAIRMAN.

I never set my sights as high as where I am today. And I have to tell you that it was never my dream to make money. My first goal was to make maybe $20,000 a year, which today might be about $65,000. That was really good.

I think we had lower expectations when I grew up. I benefited from living in the happy, post–World War II era. It was the glorious 1950s; it was about optimism and always having a pocket full of money, even if it was only fifty cents. A little bit of spending money went a long way. I mean, if you had one or two pairs of jeans and were able to go to the movies, you thought you were rich. Having a good job and a good post in the community was something to aspire to.

I went to an engineering high school because I was good at math, but I was a lousy engineer. When I graduated, I planned to study metallurgical engineering at night at New York University. **It was just luck how I got into books**. My aunt had a neighbor who was the floor manager of the New York University bookstore, so I got a job there and they paid for my tuition.

The day I started work, my provincial days as a neighborhood kid in Brooklyn were over. I was exposed to things I'd never heard of. The people who worked in the bookstore were Iranian, Indian, Chinese, African American. My first boss grew up as a farmer. I met many kinds of people I had never before encountered, and they were full of ideas and wisdom. Our paperback buyer was Hungarian and our resident Beat poet. He took one look at me and thought I was the dumbest person he'd ever met. So he gave me books I'd never been exposed to—books about economic geography, political science, psychology, and great literature. **He'd say, "Read this." I gobbled them up and thought, "Wow, the world is big."** That's sort of how I changed.

Meanwhile, I found no value in the education I was getting. I preferred to read. In my business communications class, I'd sit behind the big guys so the teacher couldn't see me reading about the Peloponnesian War! I just read and read.

At work I was what you might call a hustler. My dad taught me to work longer and harder and smarter, and I always put in extra effort. I was promoted, but I found the bookstore was too confining. I couldn't transform the store into a really great service organization. I'm naturally a person who likes to work, and I happen to like serving other people. I love doing that. But at the bookstore, I couldn't get things done.

I knew I had to do it myself, so I opened up my own store called SBX, for Student Book Exchange. It was the greatest thing I'd ever done and a great outlet. The best job in the world for me was one that I could work at eighteen hours a day. I was able to do my own thing.

We weren't revolutionary or anything. We were just an alternative to the college bookstore. Our first ad, which I created, had a picture of a red apple and it read something like, "Most college

HOW WE BOOKED IT

Mike: In college I hated studying in libraries so I did all of my homework at Starbucks or Barnes & Noble. I probably owe them rent. When we started Roadtrip Nation, one of my goals was to sit down with the big dogs from both companies. I tried to book a meeting with Len on the first trip across the country, but it didn't work out. On the second trip, we connected with people who were enthusiastic about our project. They passed on the information to Len, and he agreed to meet us.

peace, love, and books

85

bookstores do not have apples, nor do they offer a great selection, great service, and extended hours." I had 5,000 apples brought in from upstate New York and gave them to the kids who came into the store. On the first day of classes, you don't have time to eat, so I was throwing apples around!

Sure, there was mundane work. I had to ring the cash register and clean the shelves, but my mind worked all the time and I met bright people. The bookstore environment was expansive, and I had the good fortune to be doing it in the 1960s, which was a hotbed of intellectual excitement and energy. One guy who worked for me wrote " 'F' Communism" on top of a light fixture. He went on to become a director in the FBI. It was all very stimulating, and I was growing by leaps and bounds. It wasn't like I was attempting to grow—I just did.

My calling was running a good business and creating opportunities for the people who worked there. So I guess I just proceeded from that point forward to run a business with a mission of not selling products but books, the tools of education, idea tools. It's a privilege to have a job and feel like you're doing good work. We felt we were doing important work. **We also hustled like crazy**. If a student came in and needed a book for his studies, we weren't about to tell him it was out of stock.

I think I would have been somewhat successful in whatever I did. It could have been a chain of pet stores. **In those days people had ideas, not business plans**. I didn't think my ideas would rule the world, but the difference between me and others was that if you put something in front of me, I felt it was my job to explore it. When someone said to me, "You know, they need a bookstore like this at Queensborough Community

College," I'd say, "Where's Queensborough?" And we'd build there.

So that's where it all started. I think the rest of my career has been just one step after another. I felt an obligation to always take the next step. I never did it to make tons of money. That was never the dream. Today some executives think they're a failure if they don't get on the big lists or become a celebrity CEO, if the whole country doesn't envy them. I've never succumbed to those values.

Entrepreneurs have changed in the last twenty years. There's this notion that an entrepreneur is a crapshooter betting on a house of cards to make a fortune. That's baloney, a myth! An entrepreneur is a risk assessor, someone who carefully deploys assets and mitigates risk. **A good entrepreneur always knows what is going to occur and has a plan.**

Art is my latest foray. I'm the chairman of a great museum here in New York and I have to tell you that I know nothing—talk about beginning with zero knowledge. But I try to read as much as I can. It's exhilarating to reach this point in my life and realize that I have so much to learn. Every place I turn, there's a new gem. I'm lucky that my income level allows me the ultimate indulgence: knowledge for its own sake.

FILMMAKER, DOT-COM

JEHANE NOUJAIM
New York, New York
Filmmaker
Director, Startup.Com
Harvard University

JEHANE NOUJAIM'S OPEN ROAD MAP

Pre-med until tough chemistry class changes her plans;
double majors in social studies and visual and
environmental studies.

Likes anthropology and photography;
buys camera with grant money.

College internship leads to first job: works
on educational video in Boston.

Moves to New York; becomes director's assistant;
chance meeting lands job on MTV's Unfiltered.

Show cancelled; listening to roommate's plan
to start Internet company sparks documentary idea;
makes Startup.Com.

The camera gives you an excuse to go around, ask questions, and observe people.

Jehane Noujaim FOUND FAME WITH STARTUP.COM, A DOCUMENTARY FILM SHE CO-MADE ABOUT THE RISE AND FALL OF A NEW YORK–BASED INTERNET COMPANY CALLED GOVWORKS.COM. THE MOVIE CAME OUT IN MID-2001, AFTER THE SO-CALLED INTERNET BUBBLE HAD BURST. THE FILM CAPTURED THE OPTIMISM AND DEAL MAKING OF THE LATE 1990S, AND, MORE IMPORTANTLY, IT TOLD THE STORY OF THE PEOPLE BEHIND THE BUSINESS. THAT, AFTER ALL, IS WHERE THE REAL DRAMA LIES. JEHANE GOT THAT, BUT UNLIKE HER CAREER, GOVWORKS.COM NEVER TOOK OFF, AND IT WAS EVENTUALLY SOLD. WHEN WE MET WITH HER IN MANHATTAN EARLY ON A SATURDAY MORNING, SHE CURLED UP ON A SEAT IN THE RV TO RECUPERATE

AFTER A LONG NIGHT OUT WITH HER COLLEGE FRIENDS. IN A TURN OF EVENTS FOR THE FILMMAKER, SHE SAT ON THE OTHER SIDE OF THE CAMERA AND TOLD US HOW HER MOVIE—AND ROAD—CAME TO BE.

••

The first year out of college was probably the hardest year of my life. A lot of friends went into consulting or banking because they didn't know what else to do. They all had assistants and were making $60,000 a year while I was traipsing around with a little video camera. I had no idea where I was going.

I was originally studying to be a doctor because I wanted to help people around the world and travel, and I figured medicine was a body of knowledge I could use absolutely anywhere. I'm from Egypt, and I could easily go back there and be a doctor.

Then I took chemistry V and, well, that was the end of that plan. So I double majored in social studies and visual and environmental studies. People said, "Oh my God, you're majoring in both! Wow!"

Social studies was a bit of economics, a bit of statistics, and all this useful stuff that would allow me to go to law school, make a living, and have a successful career. I got the basic classes out of the way first because mom and dad said I needed them for my future life. **But visual arts was really my passion because it let me do painting, drawing, filmmaking, and photography.**

I took a lot more photography and film classes and decided

that was what I wanted to be doing. I was also really interested in anthropology, the study of people. I got into filmmaking because it's a way of learning by totally immersing yourself in an unknown world. The camera sort of gives you an excuse to go around and ask questions and observe people.

I loved being able to tell a story visually, and film let me do that more than photography could. I wanted to give voices to the people I was taking pictures of. After college I decided to give film a couple of years and see if I could make a living doing what I loved to do.

I applied for a grant, which is how I was able to buy my first camera. **Always apply for grants!** For my first job out of college a woman I'd done an internship for my sophomore year hired me to do an educational video about sustainable housing. I thought, "Okay, I have these skills, I like to shoot, I have a camera, and I'm getting paid

HOW WE BOOKED IT

Mike: Kaleil, the co-founder of GovWorks.com and the main subject of the film Startup.Com, spoke near Laguna Beach when the film was shown there. I went with Nate's mom Debbie to hear him but had to leave early. Debbie got me Kaleil's email address, and I sent him a cold request for an interview. He agreed and also suggested that we meet Jehane. So I cold called her. Not only did she agree to be interviewed, but she taught us a lot about film and the cameras that we used to film the trip. She rocks.

for it, so I'll just do this now and see where it leads me." I planned to work on the project for a year, but when the film didn't finish on time, I moved to New York and periodically went back to Boston to complete it.

You can't be unemployed for a long time in New York because it's an expensive city, so I looked around for any kind of work. I randomly sent resumes to advertising agencies and TV stations. Finally a former film teacher told me a former student, a director, was looking for an assistant. I figured I'd probably do the director's laundry for a month but it would still be the best way for me to learn about what I wanted to do. I read scripts and got to hang out with interesting people who were doing really creative work. It gave me access to a whole world that I'd never seen before and that I wanted to join.

I was not the best assistant, and I probably should have been fired three weeks into the job. But he kept me on and gave me jobs, maybe out of pity. After working for him for about a year and a half, I decided I'd learned about as much as I could.

Then, just by hanging out in New York, I met a woman named Mona who was also Egyptian and a producer. I took a job with her on a show for MTV called <u>Unfiltered</u>. We handed out cameras to kids across the United States and edited the footage they sent

TIGHT SQUEEZE

We drove around Manhattan with Jehane in the RV and hit a little glitch on a one-way street that cut through Central Park. The glitch was a tunnel. According to a sign, the tunnel was only twelve and a half feet high, but our RV was taller. We freaked out! Cars lined up behind us and honked in annoyance, but there was no way we could back up into the traffic. Then, in a stroke of genius, we got some string, climbed on top of the RV and compared its height to the height of the bridge using a piece of rope. Luckily, the sign was wrong and we had two inches to spare. Jehane, ever the documentary filmmaker, got the entire incident on tape.

us. I hadn't done much editing work, and at MTV they just throw you in an editing room. It was fascinating. The job consisted of making phone calls to kids who were really excited to tell their own stories. Some were difficult tales about heroin addiction and prostitution. One kid got kicked out of his house and was living in his car. I helped them get their stories told.

I worked there for about a year and a half, until the show got cancelled. So I had a choice: continue on at MTV or find something else. After cutting other people's footage for so long, I wanted to make my own film. I planned to go back to Egypt and make a film there.

That's when Kaleil, who had been living with me for a few months, told me he was going to quit his job at Goldman Sachs and start an Internet company that would change the way government worked. Late one night we sat down over bowls of cereal and talked about all the meetings that he was having. He told me

filmmaker, dot-com

93

how all of his friends were quitting their jobs and wanted to join him.

There was an exciting energy around what they were doing, a sense that an Internet idea could change the world. **You could hire all your friends, be your own boss, and make money, all at the same time**. I totally believed that there was a chance these guys were going to be millionaires in six months. I could even see the last shot of the film: Kaleil ringing the bell at the New York Stock Exchange. I knew nothing about business but thought it was intriguing. Egypt could wait.

The whole time I was making Startup.com I wasn't thinking it would make a name for me. I was more obsessed with telling the story and enjoying it. I was running on adrenaline. I don't think I could have concentrated on it so hard for two years if the reason I was doing it was just to get it into theaters. **There's no way you can work that hard if your heart isn't in it**.

Three years later I'm still going around promoting the film and talking about GovWorks.com. Meanwhile, Kaleil has moved on to bigger and better things.

I've really followed what's come my way and haven't done much active seeking. Sometimes I think I should be more active in pursuing what I want, but so far it's worked out pretty well.

Meanwhile, the people I know who went into consulting and banking—they had a really hard time. They made a lot of money but most of them have moved on to different professions. The analyst programs are hellish. It's so cutthroat, and they burn people out after two years.

I can't think of anything else I'd rather do. This is a constant learning process because I'm able to drop into different worlds and learn about people and the way things work.

So far my biggest sense of career fulfillment has been going to see my film on the big screen for the first time, anonymously in the dark, when nobody knew I was there. As a filmmaker, you don't really know if all the tiny decisions you made at five o'clock in the morning after drinking fifty cups of coffee are any good until you sit with an audience and hear their laughter, feel the tension, and hear their sighs. Then you think, "Wow, it worked."

GET A GRIP

BEN YOUNGER
Brooklyn, New York
Screenwriter and Director
Younger Than You Productions
Queens College, City University of New York

FIND THE OPEN ROAD

BEN YOUNGER'S OPEN ROAD MAP

↓

College internship leads to jobs in state politics; hates it.

↓

Stint on a film set solidifies his interest in movies; quits government to work as a grip on movie sets.

↓

Needs money; job interview at brokerage house sparks script idea.

↓

While writing, earns money filming corporate videos, waiting tables.

↓

Luckily, restaurant customer introduces him to agent who reads <u>Boiler Room</u> script.

↓

Refuses to sell script if he can't direct, so directs it on a small salary. <u>Boiler Room</u> released one year later; doors open.

After just one day of grabbing coffee for people, I fell in love with the film set.

Ben Younger WENT FROM WAITING TABLES TO WRITING AND DIRECTING THE FEATURE FILM BOILER ROOM, THE 2000 MOVIE ABOUT A LOST KID WHO TAKES A JOB AT A SLEAZY BROKERAGE FIRM. BEN HAS ALSO WORKED ON THOSE COOL BMW INTERNET FILMS. TO MEET BEN, WE DROVE FROM LONG ISLAND TO HIS BROOKLYN APARTMENT AT SIX IN THE MORNING, AND WE WERE EXHAUSTED. BEN HAD JUST WOKEN UP, AND WE ALL RALLIED OVER GLASSES OF ORANGE JUICE.

97

I loved movies my whole life, but I didn't think about working in the industry until I was about twenty-one, which was still pretty young. The idea of taking such a nontraditional career path was made even more unlikely for me because my family and most of the neighborhood I grew up in was modern orthodox Jewish. Having a professional career—like a lawyer or accountant—was even more important in my community. **Other career paths were actually discouraged, so it was harder for me to figure out what I wanted to do.**

During my freshman year at Queens College I had no idea where I was going. How are you supposed to know at that point? You have so little to go on. Electives are not really introductions to career paths, and it's very hard to make the connection between classes and a line of work.

My dad was an accountant, and I knew I wasn't going to do that. I majored in political science because for some reason **I decided I was going to be a lawyer. It was a real cop-out on my part, but I probably did it for lack of knowing what else to do.**

In hindsight I wish I'd taken two years off and then gone to school. I did well in college, but I didn't understand what a privilege it was. If I was in school now, I'd be loving it! It would be so easy to focus on my studies. But because college felt like an obligatory extension of high school, I didn't take it that seriously.

The guy who changed everything for me was Alan Hevesi, a

professor at Queens College and a career politician. He made politics exciting, and got me to read the Federalist Papers, on which all our freedoms and civil liberties are based.

Alan said I should work for him. When the semester ended, he was running in the primary for city comptroller, and I went from interning to being on the campaign trail, driving Alan to every meeting, watching him fund-raise, going to teamsters' meetings, trying to get everyone's support. It was amazing watching him.

He won the primary and I got a job as a policy analyst, but I started to get bored. A friend of Alan's asked me to run her campaign, so **at twenty-one I became the youngest campaign manager in New York City**. The opponent started to take shots at my candidate, really silly stuff that ended up doing some serious damage to people. The experience confirmed the fact that I didn't want to be in politics. I said, "Forget this."

Meanwhile, my buddy Phil had started to write a screenplay. It clicked. I thought, "My god, I love movies!" I started to write with Phil and to work on other projects. My girlfriend at the time had a buddy making a short film, so I went and worked as a production assistant doing grunt work. After just one day of grubbing coffee for people, I fell in love with the film set. So between that and the scriptwriting, I had found what I wanted to do.

I landed a job as a grip on a feature film, so I quit my job and sold my car. While my parents were supportive they also said, "Are you sure?" But that's the thing. I had no wife, no kids. Who cares if I lived on nothing? I ate rice and beans for the next three years, but I was happier than when I had more money and a car.

I had quit on a Friday and was supposed to start the film on a Monday, but the film—the only job I had lined up—got cancelled! The head grip knew I had quit my job and felt so bad that he brought me on a music video shoot in South Harlem. He, of course, assumed I actually knew something about being a grip, but I really knew nothing. Being on the set was like walking into an operating room and someone hands you a scalpel and says, "Here, finish the appendectomy." I barely got through the day, but I loved it. He didn't hire me again, although he became a friend.

From there I bullshitted my way onto a feature film called Walking and Talking, with Anne Heche and Catherine Keener. That's another thing. I don't want to say go out and lie, **but if you have to say whether you're qualified to do something, just say yes. My motto is say yes to everything.** I see certain people who get offered opportunities but don't think they're qualified. Just go for it! The worst-case scenario is that you screw up, which I have done so many times. But it's still fun, and you'll be amazed at what people will forgive as long as you're an amicable person and not malicious. You've got to say yes to everything.

Take Walking and Talking. The key grip called me and said he'd never heard of me, but I told him I'd been gripping for a while. Meanwhile, I'd only done it for a day on a job that I completely botched. As soon as I got a job as the third grip, I went out, got some books, and started learning everything I could.

I got to the set and the guy who was the swing—a lower position than mine—had been gripping for two years and he knew right away that I didn't know what I was doing. So I said to him, "Look, Dave, I don't know what the fuck I'm doing. I'll tell Nat [the boss] that you should be the third grip and I should be the swing. Just help me out and tell me what the hell is going on." So we did that, and he's still a friend of mine today.

From there I gripped frequently. There were some good times when I worked a lot, but I didn't have time to write because after an eighteen-hour day you're dead and can't just come home and write. And if a job came up I'd have to take it, because when you freelance you never know where your next job is coming from.

I was a waiter for a while, and I also made a short film with $17,000 of my own money. I went into debt. I was poor but happy, much happier than when I had a steady paycheck.

Two years later I still didn't know what I wanted to write about. Then a buddy said his brother was working at a brokerage house and had just bought a brand new 300ZX. The guy was younger than me! He said they were looking for recruits and that I should go check it out. So I go on the interview and knew right away that there was no way I was going to work there but, **thank God, I had found a topic to write about! I had found my film.**

It took a long time to write. I spent the next two years trying to balance work and writing. I'd interview brokers and re-search the movie whenever I could. I also started doing corporate videos with another guy. It's cake work. We'd fly around the coun-try and I'd make $1,000 a day and not have to work for another two weeks, which is when I got the writing done. Finally, the movie got written.

The corporate video work slowed, so I went back to being a waiter in Manhattan. While serving lunch to a writer named Steve one day, he asked me what I was doing. He could tell I was more than just a waiter. I told him I had made a short film and was writing a feature. He said to me, "You know what? I'm going to help you out. I feel good today." Apparently he had just come from a will reading and had inherited a ton of money.

That's another thing I believe: Talk to everyone! When I say talk I actually mean lis-ten. Too many people are concerned about making a good im-pression. Just show a bit of hunger and start asking questions. Don't stop asking questions. People like answering questions about themselves.

I'm all about asking other people what they do. And don't be afraid to ask for things. People can only say no. Asking is the del-icate part. You have to pick your moment. It's not exploitation; it's America, the land of opportunity.

With Steve I was just so friendly that he wanted to know what I did. He took my short film and watched it and sent it to his agent, telling her I was his best friend. She hated the short film, although she denies it now. [Laughs.] Seven or eight months later, I sent her the script for Boiler Room and her assistant read it, liked it, and gave it to her.

No one wanted me to direct the movie because I had no experience. **We had an offer in the high six-figures if I agreed to walk away and not direct**. The money would have gone far, but I said no. Luckily my agent was behind me. She said once I sold the movie I'd have no power. So in the end I got paid $15,000 for my script, which was still a lot for me at the time. I have pictures of the check because it signified getting paid to do what I loved. I got paid the minimum to direct it, but if I hadn't done that, I'd still be just a writer, and in Hollywood that's not a position of power.

Within a year the movie was in production. I was about twenty-five. It never happens that fast. The stars just lined up. The film opened up doors. After my movie I did two rewrites for other studios. I recently wrote a piece for The New Yorker and I do commercials, like the BMW films.

I have friends who are truly unhappy now. They got married, had a couple of kids, and are locked down. It's not that they don't love their families, but they just got into things so fast, before they figured out what they wanted to be as individuals. I think you have to be happy before you commit to having a family and such a high level of giving to other people.

If you're not married and young, you should have more than one job. Have seven or eight. What's wrong with that? Until you get married, I say take a job and quit every six months and try something new.

EYES WIDE OPEN

RICK ALLEN
Washington, D.C.
President and CEO
National Geographic Ventures
Dartmouth College

RICK ALLEN'S OPEN ROAD MAP

As marine biology major, almost fails first midterm;
switches to English.

Straight to law school after college;
hates first job until gets the nerve to change firms.

Leaves law to head company for former client;
learns about business, comfortable shouldering risk.

Helps set up AmeriCorps program
under President Clinton, a labor of love.

Back to private sector at Discovery Channel;
then National Geographic calls.

If you're in a **bad situation and can't** work it out, you can leave and life as you know it won't end.

National Geographic VENTURES IS THE FOR-PROFIT ARM OF THE NATIONAL GEOGRAPHIC SOCIETY. IN SHORT, IT'S RESPONSIBLE FOR MAKING MONEY FROM THE SOCIETY'S PRODUCTS, SUCH AS THE CABLE STATION, THE INTERNET, AND MOVIES. WHAT STRUCK US MOST ABOUT RICK'S JOURNEY WAS THAT HE HOPPED FROM ONE COOL EXPERIENCE TO THE NEXT. HE NEVER KNEW WHERE HIS NEXT GIG WAS COMING FROM. AS RICK EXPLAINS, HE WORKED HARD, KEPT HIS EYES OPEN FOR THE NEXT OPPORTUNITY, AND JUMPED WHEN IT ARRIVED. WHEN WE DROVE ONTO NATIONAL GEOGRAPHIC'S CORPORATE CAMPUS, THE BIG GREEN RV DREW

QUIZZICAL STARES FROM EMPLOYEES. BUT RICK WAS A TRUE ADVENTURER, AND HE CLIMBED ABOARD FOR THE INTERVIEW.

· ·

There is no way I could have mapped my career. A lot of it was happenstance. Back in college, I had no idea that this position even existed.

When I started college, I was passionate about marine biology. I wanted to work with dolphins. So I took a pre-med bio course my first term at Dartmouth and almost failed the midterm. I frantically thought about how I was going to get through college. I'd always loved writing and reading so I became an English major. It's one of the most interesting things I've ever done and was fabulous training.

After college I wasn't sure where I was going, but I was in a hurry to get there, so I went straight to law school. No one I knew at law school thought I'd practice it, although I did end up working as a lawyer in L.A. for about six and a half years. **My first job wasn't a good experience and, like a lot of people unhappy in their first real job, I freaked out.** I wanted to leave but thought it was too risky. Would I ever get a job again? What would it say about me as a person? Did I make the wrong career choice?

All that was nonsense. You just have to move on. Finally I jumped to another firm and loved it. It taught me that if you're in a bad situation and can't work it out, you can leave, and life as you know it won't end. It will likely get better.

At twenty-nine, my favorite client asked me to head his group of thirty-five companies. I was completely unqualified and I had not even thought about leaving law. But I did, and it turned out to be a fabulous move. Being in business is more fun than being a lawyer.

The transition was made easier for me because the fellow who hired me was brilliant, nice, and willing to bring me up to speed. Plus I knew his business because I'd been his lawyer. But the job was completely different. As a lawyer you're a consultant and get paid whether or not the business succeeds. When it's your company, you don't eat if you make too many bad choices. You're responsible for the tough calls. For some lawyers that's incredibly liberating. For others it's frightening. I did it for nine years.

Then, through a mix of circumstances, I was asked to help set up the national service program AmeriCorps under the Clinton administration. I had wanted to see a national service program since I was young, and this was an opportunity to do it. I couldn't say no.

So I went to Washington, D.C., for what was supposed to be a six-month gig. I ended up doing it for three years. I kept sticking around. Eventually I was

HOW WE BOOKED IT

Mike: We knew we wanted to interview someone from National Geographic—we just didn't know who. I skimmed the masthead of the magazine and Rick's title, CEO of National Geographic Ventures, popped out at me. I called National Geographic, asked for Rick, and was transferred to a woman who works with him. She gave me Rick's email, so I sent him a note and he replied, saying he was totally in tune with our exploration philosophy and was excited to be part of the project.

ready to go back to L.A., but I'd become friendly with the founder of the Discovery Channel and he asked me to help expand the Discovery empire. I did it for a couple years and eventually got ready to go back to California.

Then National Geographic called.

I hadn't thought about Geographic because it competed with Discovery, but the job was so unbelievably interesting and cool that I went back to my old boss at Discovery and he said, "You've got to do it." After that I could take the job with a clear conscience.

I've been here five years. The cable channel is in 134 countries, twenty-one languages, and 128 million homes worldwide. We've gotten into feature films and IMAX movies and the Web, plus maps and catalogs. We've been going full speed.

What's my advice to people entering the workforce? Have a realistic perspective on how hard it is. You may not get the exact job you want as fast as you want, or get paid as much as you deserve, **but things have a way of working out.** I bet all of the people on this ceiling [points to the roof of the RV, which is covered with signatures from people we had interviewed] have had days where everything sucked. **Being passionate about what you do doesn't mean you'll be happy all the time.** It will be tough. You will face setbacks, but if you keep pursuing your passion seriously, things will happen that you can't predict.

EARLY BLOOMER

DEB CALLAHAN
Washington, D.C.
President
League of Conservation Voters
University of California, Santa Barbara

DEB CALLAHAN'S OPEN ROAD MAP

↓

Young Deb loves nature, decides to
champion environment through politics.

↓

Stays the course: starts high school recycling programs;
studies forestry and biology in college.

↓

Disheartened until she transfers to an
environmental studies program.

↓

No jobs when she graduates; starts grad school.

↓

Leaps at chance to work on presidential campaign;
"politics sucks you in."

↓

Travels for years doing campaigns until gets job
she dreamed of as little girl, heading
League of Conservation Voters.

Listen to yourself and know what you really want.
You can't ever go back in time.

The League OF CONSERVATION VOTERS IS A 40,000-MEMBER NATIONAL ORGANIZATION THAT WORKS TO MAKE SURE CONGRESS PASSES ENVIRONMENTALLY FRIENDLY LAWS. IT ALSO HELPS ELECT CANDIDATES AND DEFEAT THOSE WITH ANTI-ENVIRONMENT PLATFORMS. RUNNING THE LEAGUE IS A LIFELONG DREAM FOR DEB. SHE'S GROWN INTO A SAVVY POLITICAL OPERATIVE WHO HAS ALWAYS BEEN PASSIONATE ABOUT THE ENVIRONMENTAL MOVEMENT. SITTING ON THE COUCH IN HER OFFICE—LOCATED IN THE HUB OF D.C.—SHE EXPLAINED, "IT'S NOT A MOVEMENT IF YOU JUST SIT STILL. YOU HAVE TO KEEP MOVING FORWARD."

I'm a funny bird because I knew what I wanted to do at an early age. Plus, my parents never lost faith, and it was important to have people who believed in me.

I grew up in Southern California, and we had a cabin in Big Bear. I would go off with my dog and explore the woods. **I came to love nature.** We also lived in Los Angeles, which in those days was much more polluted. So I saw the two extremes: the beauty and the beast of what the environment could be. My parents belonged to environmental organizations and we'd get these newsletters that always said, "Write your congressman!" **At a young age, I figured out that if you want to save the Earth you have to get political.**

When I was twelve I realized that I wanted to go into environmental politics and I focused on it. In high school I started a nonprofit recycling center. When I got to college in 1976, there weren't majors in environmental activism, so I started in a traditional school of forestry at California Polytechnic State University, San Luis Obispo. It took me two and a half years to figure out that forestry was about cutting trees down, not keeping them up. [Laughs.]

So I transferred to the school of biology and dissected every possible creature. Then, I went to the University of California in Santa Barbara and majored in environmental studies and minored in political science. By the time I graduated, I had many different perspectives: science, forestry, politics, even theater.

I got out of school and thought, "Hey world, here I am!" But there were no jobs for me.

Because of my theater background, I was offered a spot as an assistant producer, which is a very cool career. But I decided to stick with what was important to me. It's key that you listen to yourself and know what you really want. You can't ever go back in time, and some choices are harder to make when you're older. **So ask yourself, "What can't I do when I'm encumbered with family and homeownership?"**

In 1981 I interned at the National Clean Air Coalition in Washington. After about three months I went back to Los Angeles, but three years later I still couldn't find anything. I was frustrated. Meanwhile, I took graduate classes at UCLA and was thinking about law school. I even worked at a corporate law firm for a year.

HOW WE BOOKED IT

When we were visiting George Washington University, we met a student interested in environmental law. She told us we should interview the queen of the environmental world, Deb Callahan, who headed the League of Conservation Voters. We dialed information, got the organization's number, and explained the project to one of Deb's colleagues. She was psyched about it, and we met with Deb a few days later.

Then, in January 1984, I got a phone call from a guy who I'd interned with at the Clean Air Coalition. He was in Iowa organizing the presidential campaign for Walter Mondale and asked if I'd come work with him. He said he needed me in two days. I wasn't sure, but I believed then, as I do now, that you should take an opportunity when it's presented to you. You never know where it might lead. **So in the next two days I dropped out of school, quit my job, left my boyfriend, and went to Iowa for what I thought would be a month.**

But politics kind of sucks you in. I did a good job, and they sent me to New Hampshire, then Wyoming. When the campaign finally ended, a year had passed and I'd organized campaigns in eight states, plus worked on the Democratic National Convention. I never moved back to L.A.

Afterward I got my first job with an environmental organization in New Hampshire, where I was regional political director for the League of Conservation Voters. I began to move around the country, working on campaigns. In nonelection years I did environmental lobbying. Consequently, I lived in about twenty different states until I moved back to Washington, D.C., for this job.

Today I run the organization that handles environmental politics for the whole environmental movement. I use every scrap of what I've learned along the way, even theater. I do a lot of public speaking. In fact, politics is theater. You're playing a role. And I happen to like to talk, so politics is a good fit for me.

Certainly there have been tough times. Politics is a contact sport. It takes so much energy and commitment and you get beaten up. Powerful people don't like to be messed with. When members of Congress take a hit, they hit back.

Also, campaign organizers have no guaranteed employment, and after election day there's nothing for you to do. One thing I regret is not finishing my master's degree because someday I'd like to teach college. But once you're mid-career, it's really hard to go back and get an advanced degree. On the other hand, you should never get an advanced degree just because you don't know what else to do.

I didn't get into this business to get rich. I made ends meet along the way but there were sacrifices. Sometime I kept the wolves at bay when it came to rent. [Laughs.] But I'm much more financially stable now.

I was lucky. I knew when I was twelve what made me happy. I got the job of my dreams so much earlier than I ever imagined. I don't know where I'll go from here.

early bloomer

PURSE DUTY

MORRIS REID
Washington, D.C.
Lobbyist, Westin Rinehart
University of Akron

MORRIS REID'S OPEN ROAD MAP

Gravitates to behind-the-scenes political work; does PR work in college.

Client gets him involved with Bill Clinton's presidential campaign.

Works for First Lady in D.C. but "aggressive" networking soon lands him job with his idol, Commerce Secretary Ronald Brown.

Works hard on old-lady "purse duty" and excels to secretary's aide.

Trip to Bosnia ends in tragic death of Ron Brown and fellow staffers.

Commits to succeeding; works hard; thrives as lobbyist and consultant.

No job is too small.

In April 1996, THE U.S. SECRETARY OF COMMERCE, RON BROWN, WAS ON AN AIR FORCE PLANE THAT CRASHED INTO THE MOUNTAINS A FEW MILES FROM DUBROVNIK, CROATIA. TRAVELING WITH SECRETARY BROWN WERE THIRTY-FOUR PEOPLE, INCLUDING BUSINESS EXECUTIVES AND COLLEAGUES. WHILE THERE WAS ONLY ONE SURVIVOR FOUND AT THE CRASH, THERE WAS SOMEONE ELSE CLOSE TO BROWN WHO WAS NOT ON THE PLANE THAT DAY. THAT PERSON WAS THE SECRETARY'S PERSONAL AIDE, MORRIS REID. TODAY, MORRIS IS THIRTY YEARS OLD AND WORKS AS A GOVERNMENT LOBBYIST AND BUSINESS CONSULTANT. BEFORE THE TRAGEDY, MORRIS HAD PAVED HIS ROAD INTO POLITICS BY BEING AGGRESSIVE AND

HARDWORKING. SINCE THEN HE HAS DOUBLED HIS EFFORTS. AFTER ALL, HE SAYS, HE'S LIVING LIFE FOR THIRTY-THREE PEOPLE WHO NO LONGER CAN.

I didn't come from an affluent background and had no appreciation for school. I was very unfocused. The day I arrived at the University of Akron, I knew I wanted to get out as quickly as possible, because there was a whole world I wanted to see.

My grandmother's accident led me to politics. She got injured and I had to get her Social Security and things of that nature, which meant I had to call up congressmen. The whole experience led to a career path of walking up to people who I didn't know, talking to them, seeking advice, and picking their brains.

I didn't want to be a politician because they really don't make that much money, so I figured out how to use politics to get to the money. In college I started a little PR company that represented politicians. I made $1,000 a week and was the richest guy on campus. My break came when I was working for a state representative who happened to be from Arkansas. He said a guy named Bill Clinton was going

HOW WE BOOKED IT

Networking was a big help landing a meeting with Morris. Everyone we interviewed knew someone else we should meet, and we were actually referred to Morris by the colleague of another entrepreneur we'd met. We simply phoned Morris and said that his publicist referred us.

to run for president and he might be able to get me hooked into the campaign.

To make a long story short, I ended up running a portion of the northeast Ohio campaign for Clinton. I got exposed to all the principals, like Bill and Hillary, Al and Tipper Gore. Meanwhile, they saw this young guy who was hungry and aggressive and doing what he needed to do. **Being hungry and aggressive paid off, especially the aggressive part.**

After Clinton was elected, Hillary's people called me and asked me to come to D.C. and work for them. I packed everything I had into a duffel bag and jumped on a Greyhound bus from Akron to Washington.

The day I arrived I knew I wanted to work with Ron Brown. I asked everyone if they knew him or knew someone who knew him. Eventually, I found three people, and we identified a person named Mike who could get me a job: Mike was the chief of staff for the inaugural committee. I asked people to talk to Mike about me. Then one day I walked into his office and said, "Hi, I'm Morris Reid. I know a lot of people have been bugging you about me." Mike said he couldn't use me, so I told him I just wanted to introduce myself and asked him to let me know if anything happened.

A few days later I told a friend of mine who worked for Hillary Clinton that I really appreciated all she had done for me but that I wanted to work for Ron Brown. Unbeknownst to me, she called Mike and said that I was already on her payroll, but that if I worked for both of them, Mike wouldn't have to pay me. Two days later Mike called me. I was ecstatic. He said, "Reid, your job is to take care of Ron Brown's mother and mother-in-law." [Laughs.]

It was the best thing that had happened to me. Here I was on "purse duty," a phrase I coined, for a couple of old ladies. My job was to get them from one place to another, carry their purses, help them along. **It was the biggest break of my life** because these two little old black women saw this young black kid who was ecstatic about everything. And these women talked about me nonstop! Nonstop! So Secretary Brown wondered, "Who the hell is this kid Morris Reid?" That's my point: No job is too small. There I was, on purse duty carrying a Chanel bag—and it didn't even match my outfit! [Laughs.]

One day I was at an event and something went wrong. Being aggressive, I jumped in and fixed it. Later, Mike told me I'd done a great job and asked me to join him at the Washington Convention Center that night. I went and was made the coat man for the

THE JOYS OF PARKING

Mike: I almost got into a fight minutes before our interview with Morris. First, you have to understand how difficult it is to park a forty-foot RV in a crowded city like downtown Washington, D.C. So when we spotted four empty parking spots next to each other, it was a miracle! I jumped out of the RV and stood in the spots to save them until the RV turned the corner. Suddenly a big black Lincoln Navigator pulled into one of the spots I was saving. I didn't move my body and the truck kept heading toward me. I put my hands on the bumper and actually started to push it. The driver started yelling at me, and I lost it. I just snapped. I went on about how hard it was to park a forty-foot RV. He had no idea what the hell I was talking about until the blue-and-green rig showed up, and then he promised to leave if I apologized for assaulting his car. I did and he took off. Bigger bummer: After several tries to park the monster, we realized the space was actually too small.

evening. So I'm standing in the corner holding everyone's coats, and President Clinton comes by and says, "Hey, Morris." Secretary Brown looks at me like, "Who the hell is this kid?" [Laughs.] That evening Secretary Brown's son offered me a job to work with his dad.

I went from being Secretary Brown's gofer to his personal assistant. I drove around with him and his wife, and I was the fly on the wall in every meeting he had. I was the first person he saw in the morning and the last person he saw at night. I was a young aide, but I spent so much time with him that he'd tell me things he couldn't say to other people. He relied on me. People at the Commerce Department used to call me a "leading indicator," because they knew what Brown was going to do based on my attitude.

This was a lot of power for a young kid from Akron, Ohio, and

I often screwed up. Brown fired me twelve times, but I'd show up the next day. We had such a fantastic relationship. **He was more than a boss—he was my mentor.**

We were on a trip to Croatia and I was supposed to be with Secretary Brown on a plane to Dubrovnik. It was a trip I told him he had to take because it was important. He wanted me to stay behind in another city and focus on a deal we were doing. When he saw me sitting on the plane he said, "I thought I told you I didn't want you on this trip." They literally had to roll back the stairs to the plane so I could get off.

Later I flew down separately to meet him. An hour and thirty minutes before the secretary's plane was supposed to land, it disappeared from the radar. We learned several hours later that the plane had crashed.

I flew home on a C-17 with five other people and thirty-three bodies. The aircraft was gutted and it was just me and thirty-three coffins, including my mentor and all of my friends. This was my world, and they were all dead and I really felt like I was the reason. I was the guy who was directing what he did. I had insisted he go to Dubrovnik. **We flew back home for twelve hours, and it was the most horrific experience of my life.** I was twenty-six.

My friends always ask if I'm over it. No. I never want to be over it because it's become the driving force of my life. Here was a guy in his fifties and others in their thirties and forties—they all had long lives to live. I never want to forget that pain. It propels me. I feel like I'm living a certain part of my life devoted to making sure I'm a success. Secretary Brown would have been a success, so I want to continue to do things my friends never got to do. I feel every day that I have a new lease on life, a day that I wasn't supposed to have. It's hard for me to have a bad day because nothing will ever equal that pain.

Now I try to focus on running my business. I've started one company and am a major player in two others. I leave my house every morning at 7:15 and come home at 11:30 every night. I put in a full day, and at the end of it I look at what I accomplished. **I'm very critical of myself, but it keeps me sharp.** It's a day-to-day, week-to-week measurement. It's almost like flying an airplane: You have to watch the instruments and know what's going on with the plane moment to moment because if anything goes wrong, the plane could crash.

CARTOON CHARACTER

MIKE LAZZO
Atlanta, Georgia
Senior Vice President, Programming and
Production
Cartoon Network
Never attended college

MIKE LAZZO'S OPEN ROAD MAP

⬇

Bucks expectations: says no to college
and dad's textile industry.

⬇

Enjoys watching, critiquing TV. "Dawns on me
to get a job...at a television network."

⬇

Picks mailroom in "nutty" cable company,
Turner Broadcasting.

⬇

Meets employees while delivering mail;
exposed to programming department.

⬇

Epiphany: "I could actually get paid to watch TV
and have an opinion."

⬇

Daily reality check: If manual labor looks better
than what he's doing, that's when he'll quit.

I took a massive pay cut to deliver mail.

Mike Lazzo GETS PAID TO WATCH TELEVISION. HE ALSO GETS PAID TO DECIDE WHAT OTHER PEOPLE WILL WATCH. ALTHOUGH IT SOUNDS CLICHÉ, HE REALLY DID GET HIS START DELIVERING MAIL AT THE CABLE STATION. AS A KID HE WAS EXTREMELY LOST, BUT HE HAD THE SENSE TO IDENTIFY WHAT HE LOVED—TELEVISION—AND THE PATIENCE TO START AT THE BOTTOM. WALKING THROUGH THE HALLWAYS OF THE CARTOON NETWORK IS LIKE BEING INSIDE A CARTOON. HUGE DRAWINGS OF THE FLINTSTONES AND POWERPUFF GIRLS COVER THE WALLS. IT'S A FANTASY WORK ENVIRONMENT THAT SUITS MIKE WHO, WITH HIS LONG HAIR TIED BACK IN TWO SHORT BRAIDS, FEELS RIGHT AT HOME.

When I was fifteen years old, I ran away from home with a friend to go see the rock band Yes. But we missed the guy who was supposed to drive us to the concert and ended up spending the night at an abandoned house. Ten years later, when I was interviewing at Turner Broadcasting Systems, I looked out the window and saw that same house. It had been turned into the station's studio! So there was a little bit of kismet involved. You have to look for signs, because they're out there.

I had no direction when I was in high school. I was expected to go to college or to work in the textile industry like my father had done. But I just couldn't do it because it was too boring. So for a while I did a series of odd jobs—I worked in a music store, made sandwiches—none of which was gratifying. At night I did what I really wanted to do: watch televi-sion, think about it, and bore people with my opinions.

Look, you never walk into your dream job right off the bat. When I started at the network I delivered mail. I'd been working at a movie theater and watching a lot of TV—Cheers, Hill Street Blues—and it slowly dawned on me that maybe I'd just get a job in the mailroom at a television network. I thought it was important to be close to my natural interest. I took a massive pay cut to deliver mail. They could have told me I'd be digging holes; as long as there were TV monitors in the vicinity, I would have been happy.

There were lots of TV networks, but there was something about Turner Broadcasting. It was one of the very first cable channels, and it seemed eccentric, a little nutty. I responded to that.

Delivering mail turned out to be the best job in the world be-cause I got to know everybody at the company. I knew who was

SPEED RACER

Mike Lazzo not only agreed to sign the ceiling of the RV, he also wanted to drive the rig to his car, which was parked in a faraway lot. Keep in mind that a thirty-one-foot recreational vehicle drives much differently than a regular car, but we don't think that fact occurred to Mike. He hit the gas and floored it, tearing around corners. We thought we would die, or at least topple over. We made it to his car in one piece, then Mike Lazzo pulled into a parking space front first. After we dropped him off, it took us about a half hour to back the RV out!

helpful and who was not. At first I thought I wanted to work in audio production, but the biggest asshole you've ever seen ran that area and I didn't want to work for him. [Laughs.] By listening to people in the programming department, I realized that, hey, I could get paid to decide what movie would play on Tuesday night. It was already my hobby! I could actually get paid to watch TV and have an opinion.

So ask yourself: "What's my hobby? What would I do for free? What would I pay people to let me do?" There's always something, that thing that you would do for no money. Identify that and you've found your perfect job, if you're willing to work at it. My ability to work hard definitely helped me, but natural interest is what keeps people getting out of bed. There are people out there who truly are born to be lawyers and doctors. Let them be lawyers and doctors. That wasn't me.

I have two litmus tests for my work. If I drive by a construction site and want to start digging because manual labor seems more satisfying than my current job, then that's a sign it's time to switch jobs. The other test I do is this: Every single day I ask myself if I'm happy. The day I say no is the day I leave.

COLLEGE CAN WAIT

MICHAEL DELL
Austin, Texas
Dell Computer Corp.
Founder and CEO
University of Texas;
dropped out after freshman year

MICHAEL DELL'S OPEN ROAD MAP

Considers becoming a doctor, majors in biology.

Burgeoning computer industry captures his attention.

Drops out of college without telling parents.

Starts mail-order computer business that takes off;
parents forgive him for leaving college;
he never returns to school.

Don't be afraid to fail
because that's usually when you learn.

Michael Dell IS PERHAPS BEST KNOWN FOR CHANGING THE WAY PERSONAL COMPUTERS (PCs) ARE SOLD. WHILE OTHER COMPANIES WERE BUILDING PCs AND SELLING THEM THROUGH STORES, DELL REVERSED THE MODEL. THE COMPANY CUSTOM-BUILDS PCs AND SHIPS THEM DIRECTLY TO INDIVIDUAL USERS. ITS MODEL WORKED, AND IT HAS MADE MICHAEL DELL ONE OF THE WORLD'S WEALTHIEST PEOPLE. NO WONDER TWO SECURITY GUARDS REFUSED TO LET US INTO DELL'S PARKING LOT UNTIL HIS ASSISTANT CONFIRMED WITH THEM THAT THE SCRUBS IN THE GREEN RV REALLY WERE THERE TO SEE MICHAEL DELL.

My parents weren't very happy when I decided to drop out of college. My father was a doctor, my grandfather was a doctor, and while my parents didn't say I had to be a doctor, it just seemed like a good idea at the time. I didn't really see myself as a guy going to a big company. Plus, I was pretty good at math and science.

I majored in biology but as a freshman got very excited about computers. I saw an incredible opportunity in the business. My parents and I went through a time when we talked about my dropping out. They thought it was a very bad idea. You know, they said

all this stuff like, "You've got to get your priorities straight," and "What's going to become of you?" [Laughs.] Eventually I decided that there was no way they'd accept it, **so I dropped out without telling them**. That's the only way it seemed to make sense.

After a while they got over it. It helped that I started the company right away and that it took off very quickly. I also knew that if the company didn't take off, I could go back to school. **It wasn't like college would not be there in another six months or a year**. The worst thing that could have happened, I thought, was that I'd learn something.

When you "go for it," you learn what you're capable of. I tell people not to be afraid to fail because that's usually when you learn. And when you're starting a new business, you have incredible opportunities to fail.

I wouldn't say I was nervous. I was more intense and naive. I didn't know all kinds of things, but that turned out to be a strength. The great thing about the technology world is that things are changing all the time. People who come into the industry have an opportunity to create new businesses because they're not encumbered by past ideas. Not being

HOW WE BOOKED IT

Nate: It took two years of creative faxes, emails, and phone calls before we were allowed to meet Michael Dell. I was bumped from one division to another until I got so frustrated that I called the main number and asked to speak directly with Michael Dell. I was transferred to Laura, a woman in his office who was upbeat about our project. I stayed in touch with Laura as we planned trip number two. After convincing Dell's public relations department that, yes, we would show up on time and no, we wouldn't ask Michael crazy questions, we eventually got a meeting. We weren't the only ones trying to get face time with him. When we arrived at Dell's offices, a slew of television reporters were waiting outside hoping to interview Michael on camera. Imagine their surprise when the billion-dollar man disappeared inside a mangy RV to chat with a bunch of scrubs.

bound by conventional wisdom can be extremely helpful.

I wouldn't have done well at a place where I had to conform. People say to me today, "You're the CEO. You've gotta play golf." **But I don't want to play golf.** I know that refusing to play golf is not some big, nonconformist behavior, but I don't do a lot of things because people want me to do them.

Everyone has their own definition of success. For me it's happiness. That's the most important thing. Do I enjoy what I'm doing? Do I enjoy the people I'm doing it with? Do I have time to be with my family and do things I like? That's what it's all about. **Unfortunately, a lot of people conform and go through life being unhappy.** If you find yourself in that situation, do everything you can to get out of it. If you're in a place where creative thinking isn't appreciated, maybe you should go to a different place.

STIR THE ENTREPRENEUR WITHIN

HOWARD SCHULTZ
Seattle, Washington
Chairman, Starbucks Coffee Co.
Owner, Seattle SuperSonics
Northern Michigan University

HOWARD SCHULTZ'S OPEN ROAD MAP

Grows up in housing projects in Brooklyn, New York.

Plays college football on scholarship.

Graduates and works for Xerox; learns about business.

Takes job as head of Starbucks' marketing in Seattle.

Travels to Italy, where he discovers a passion
for Italian espresso bars.

Barely raises money to buy Starbucks' six stores and
pursues dream of importing Italian coffee culture
to the United States.

I wanted to build a company that my father never got a chance to work for.

Howard's story IS THE EPITOME OF THE AMERICAN DREAM. HE GREW UP IN BROOKLYN'S HOUSING PROJECTS AND TODAY RUNS A $2.6 BILLION BUSINESS THAT HAS CHANGED THE WAY THE WORLD DRINKS COFFEE. HE HAD GREAT IDEAS AND SOLID TRAINING AND WAS WISE ENOUGH TO SURROUND HIMSELF WITH SMART, PASSIONATE PEOPLE. AT STARBUCKS' HEADQUARTERS IN SEATTLE, WE SANK INTO COZY CHAIRS AND DRANK MUGS OF STARBUCKS COFFEE WHILE CHATTING WITH HOWARD. IT WAS JUST LIKE BEING IN, WELL, A STARBUCKS.

I've always been a big risk taker, although I don't know where that comes from. I literally grew up in federally subsidized housing in New York. Not only was my neighborhood on the other side of the tracks, but it was <u>way</u> on the other side.

My dad never made more than $20,000 a year. I watched him have one bad blue-collar job after another. Not only wasn't he valued, but he was disrespected. There was a lot of angst around financial problems, and I was concerned about whether that was going to happen to me. **But I remember my mother telling me at an early age that I could do anything in this country.** All that probably gave me a unique entrepreneurial drive to enhance my standing in life. I didn't want to be part of that class of people that didn't have access to the American dream.

Yet I was totally displaced. I had no idea what I would do. I had fear and trepidation and insecurity about how it would all turn out.

I went to Northern Michigan University to play football. That was the only

HOW WE BOOKED IT

Mike: In college I spent a lot of time studying at a local Starbucks and it became my mission to meet the man who started the company. We tried, unsuccessfully, to interview him on our first roadtrip. But Howard was also on the road that summer and our paths never crossed. We were determined to meet him on the second roadtrip. Luckily a friend of mine knew someone who worked in the marketing department. I met her for coffee, and she introduced me to another woman who worked closely with Howard. She understood what we were all about and tried to set up an interview but didn't confirm anything until a week before we were scheduled to be in Seattle. When we finally sat down with him, a PR rep asked Howard if he knew that we had been trying to book a meeting with him for two years. He looked over at me and said, "What took you so long?"

way I could have gotten to college. I wasn't very good. When I finished school, I went to work for Xerox from 1976 to 1979. It wasn't a company I thought I would ever stay with, but it gave me self-confidence and great training.

Most entrepreneurs benefit greatly by working in an environment where they can see how a company works, where they can see processes and how decisions get made and can get training that builds a foundation. Entrepreneurs who try to do too much too early can have trouble attaining the kind of success that would be more assured if they had more experience. Xerox prepared me. It was great and imprinted on me a certain knowledge.

For a few years after Xerox, I managed the introduction of a Swedish housewares company in New York. I always knew in my heart that I was going to try to do something myself. I didn't know what, but when I was traveling in Europe, **I discovered the romance of the Italian espresso bar in Italy. It was an epiphany for me. It was something I just felt intuitively**.

There seems to be an erosion of using one's intuition. There is so much data, information, research, and quantitative stuff. I think you should trust your intuition and not fear it. Allow it to manifest itself, balanced with training, education, and analysis.

I also started thinking about whether it was possible to create an organization that valued the human spirit. Is it possible to achieve a balance between fiscal responsibility and developing shareholder value while at the same time leading with your heart and having a conscience as a company? A lot of that had to do with watching my dad and seeing the effect his work had on his life and our family. I wanted to build a company that my father never got a chance to work for.

I moved to Seattle as head of Starbucks' marketing in 1982 and eventually I acquired the company's six stores for $3.8 million in 1987. I had no money to my name and had to go out and do that through investors. **The first year I tried to raise equity for the business, I talked to 240 people and 99 percent of them said no.** My wife was pregnant with our first child and it was a brutal time. It was very, very hard.

Have the courage to dream big. Don't allow anyone to tell you or convince you that your dreams can't come true. So much of building a successful business is about taking the road less traveled and having a core group of people believing when so many others don't. I don't think that you can be successful on your own without an unbridled love and enthusiasm for doing something you really, really love. You can't fake it for long. People will see through it.

We said we're going to build a company that redefines coffee in America, and we're going to have Italian names on the coffee that no one can pronounce. So twenty years later, we are about to open store number 5,000. We serve 20 million customers a week in more than thirty countries.

There are so many older people out there who are bitter and angry at the world. But at the end of the day, they are angry with themselves because they didn't follow their dreams. But it is too late for them to change because, perhaps, their level of expense has grown to their level of income and they can't get out of it. They sacrificed and they settled and woke up one day and realized that theirs was a life about mediocrity.

So ask yourself, "What are my dreams?" Define your aspirations. Then try to create a path so you are walking and working toward something. You need a little luck and good timing, but **the difference between success and failure is this gray line between will, passion, and self-belief that "I'm going to do this."**

Can you achieve your dream if it is financially driven? Perhaps in the short term, but it won't be sustainable because it's shallow. It will not fill your heart. It will not fill your life.

SONICS TICKETS, ANYONE?

After our talk with Howard, he looked at us and said, "You know what you guys need?" "Yeah," we thought, "a shower." But Howard had something else in mind. "You need tickets to the Sonics game tonight." We were so fired up! That night we found ourselves in a packed stadium and could see Howard cheering from his courtside seat. Unfortunately, the Sonics lost. No problem! We still had a blast.

BEER PIONEER

PAUL SHIPMAN
Woodinville, Washington
Founder and CEO
Redhook Ale Brewery
Bucknell University

PAUL SHIPMAN'S OPEN ROAD MAP

Goes to Bucknell expecting to be a lawyer like
his father and grandfather.

Junior year in France sparks the entrepreneur within;
decides to bring European-style alcoholic beverages
to the United States.

Works for winery but needs more training;
off to business school.

Meets Gordon Bowker, "the catalyst," who pushes Paul
to start one of the first microbreweries.

First beer sold in 1982; spends early years battling
lack of consumer interest and later years
fighting competitors.

The most harrowing experience I've ever had was starting this company.

Redhook WAS ONE OF THE FIRST MICROBREWED BEERS TO HIT AMERICA BACK IN 1982. IT TOOK A WHILE FOR PEOPLE TO ACCEPT THE NEW, BELGIAN-INSPIRED SPICY BREW, BUT THE FLAVORS CAUGHT ON. IN THE YEARS SINCE, HUNDREDS OF SMALL BREWERIES HAVE SPRUNG UP TO COMPETE WITH REDHOOK. BUT COFOUNDER PAUL SHIPMAN HAS HUNG ON AND REMAINS CHIEF EXECUTIVE. THERE'S A GREAT SIGN OUTSIDE OF REDHOOK'S HEAD-QUARTERS THAT DEFINES THE ESSENCE OF PAUL: "WE DO NOT ALL HAVE THE PRIVILEGE OF BEING ATHLETES, POETS, AND STATESMEN. BUT ONE QUALITY BINDS US ALL. WE ARE BEER DRINKERS." WE MET PAUL IN THE CROWDED TROLLEYMAN PUB THAT IS ACTUALLY LOCATED INSIDE REDHOOK'S CORPORATE

HEADQUARTERS. HE ORDERED US ALL A ROUND OF PITCHERS, AND THEN AN-
OTHER ROUND. LUCKILY, IT WAS OUR LAST INTERVIEW OF THE DAY.

．．

There are two periods in life when you're most likely to start a business. First, in your late twenties. You have boundless energy and you haven't been knocked around enough to know how tough business can be. You look at things that seem impossible to someone older and, instead of giving up, you just do it. The other pivotal period is your early forties. You no longer have boundless energy, but you still have enough, plus you have a degree of wisdom and you've been knocked around a bit, so you're more cautious. There's better planning.

I started Redhook in my late twenties.

I was supposed to be a lawyer. Almost everyone in my high school class went on to college. We were all very ambitious, and in our little town kids were expected to be outstanding in every way.

I went to Bucknell University, a fairly small school on the East Coast. My father had gone to Bucknell and become a lawyer, and his father went to Bucknell and became a lawyer, too. So there was a very clear expectation in my mind and in everyone else's mind that I would go to law school. Nobody even asked me. I was sort of born to it.

But I had a defining experience in my junior year. I studied in France, which was uncommon in those days. I think I was the only one in my class who went to Europe. It was exotic, but academically it was a breeze. [Laughs.] I don't think I would be the same person if I had not gone to France. Everyone should spend time in a foreign country.

I came back to the country after a year and concluded that part of my mission would be to bring a new dimension to life in the United States. Already I was thinking about alcoholic beverages. In Europe, people have a more casual relationship with alcohol. They never had Prohibition, and they have excellent products that are consumed, basically, most of the day. That was not the case in the United States, especially in the 1970s.

That plan replaced my idea of becoming a lawyer, so I went to work selling wine for a small winery in Pennsylvania. It was fun, but I realized that I needed more professional training from business school. Unfortunately, I had not been an outstanding college student, so I had to bear down to get a high score on my GMAT. I just dug in, did very well, and went to the University of Virginia, which in those days was not that hard to get into. It was a lucky break.

The guys at school in-

HOW WE BOOKED IT

Mike: One day in Barnes & Noble, I came across a book titled Beer Pioneer. It was all about how Paul Shipman founded Redhook Ale and essentially invented the microbrew industry. I read it cover to cover in the bookstore, in one sitting. I was so intrigued that I "pulled a 411" to get Redhook's corporate number. I phoned and asked for Paul's office and left a message on his voice mail. He's one of the few CEOs who actually answers his own phone. Paul called me back the next day. We sat down with him on our first roadtrip and caught up with him again on the second.

troduced me to people in Seattle's wine business. I made an effort to get to know many businesspeople; I had no time for bullshitters. One guy I got to know eventually became my business partner, Gordon Bowker. He was the catalyst. If I didn't have him, Redhook might not have happened when or how it did.

The most harrowing experience I've ever had was starting this company. It was more intense than flying airplanes or being in a foreign country where I couldn't speak the language. I can't imagine anyone doing it easily. **It's hell**. There were no microbreweries, and the first thing investors always asked was, "Who else has done this?" At the time no one had done precisely what we were going to do.

The five-year period between 1991 and 1996 was a time of concentrated output. It was the peak of my career. I built two breweries, looked for venture capital, had a public stock offering, reorganized the board of directors, did the deal with Anheuser-Busch, and went to national distribution. I know there won't be another five-year period like that in my future.

We tried to leap ahead of the fragmented market, like Starbucks did, but our competition was simultaneously supercharged. We really didn't think so many people would follow us. Now the microbrewery industry is in a shakeout. It's a war of attrition, and I don't know if I would have started the business if I'd known that was going to happen.

If you want to be an entrepreneur, you must have a strong sense of independence. It's a human thing to want to belong, but entrepreneurs can't worry about that. When people leave school and go into the real world, they're usually in an organization of some kind—maybe a law firm, maybe government, a company, a hospital, who knows. **Don't become too much a part of the organization because it can anesthetize you**. Why? Most people want to belong. But successful entrepreneurs don't have that as their driver, in my opinion.

This is what I say to people who want to start something from scratch: The world is getting along just fine without your thing, whatever it is. The world will continue to get along without that thing. When you impose your thing upon the world, you're trying to change the status quo. In Redhook's case we were trying to change the beer business. The imported beers were doing pretty much what we wanted to do—providing a different flavor. The world could have gotten along just fine without microbreweries, but it's better with them.

I love my beers. Developing new products is my new favorite thing. When I was younger, I was content to delegate product development. Now I'm much more involved. I still get excited about coming to work even though I don't jump out of bed as fast as when I was in my thirties.

beer pioneer

SOLE OF AN ARCHITECT

TINKER HATFIELD
Beaverton, Oregon
Vice President of Design and Special Projects
Nike
University of Oregon

TINKER HATFIELD'S OPEN ROAD MAP

Small-town jock gets hurt in college;
"dug into" his architecture studies.

Graduates, gets architect's license but
"not quite sure what to do."

Job as Nike's store architect combines design
skills and love of sports.

Transitions into shoe design; thrives
in competitive environment.

Designs first Michael Jordan basketball shoe,
and the next twelve.

These days prefers role of mentor and
"making himself useful."

The more experiences you have,
the easier it is to connect the dots later in life.

Tinker Hatfield HAS WORKED WITH MICHAEL JORDAN
AND LED DESIGN TEAMS THAT CREATED THIRTEEN DIFFERENT VERSIONS OF
THE AIR JORDAN BASKETBALL SHOE. NIKE'S HEADQUARTERS LOOKS LIKE A
COLLEGE CAMPUS. THE BUILDINGS, CLUSTERED AROUND A LAKE, ARE NAMED
AFTER FAMOUS ATHLETES. WE MET TINKER ON THE GROUND FLOOR OF THE
MIA HAMM BUILDING, WHERE HE WORKS IN A PLACE APTLY CALLED THE
"INNOVATION KITCHEN." THIS IS WHERE SPECIAL PRODUCTS, LIKE AIR
JORDANS, ARE COOKED UP. TINKER'S ROAD IS A GREAT EXAMPLE OF HOW

DIFFERENT PARTS OF ONE'S LIFE CAN COME TOGETHER IN UNANTICIPATED WAYS. IN HIS CASE, A CHILDHOOD LOVE OF SPORTS MESHED WITH ARCHITECTURE.

Well, I'm from a small town where there weren't a lot of choices. You either worked on the farms or participated in sports. I was just a jock. My dad was a coach. My mom was a coach. My sister married a coach and my brother was a coach. Sports was the center of our lives, so I played football and basketball and ran track in high school.

I had dreamed of being a professional athlete of some sort, but for the majority of people that's just not realistic. I had some success and actually competed in track and field at the University of Oregon, where I went on a scholarship. But in my second year of college, I figured out that sports was not what I'd be doing for the rest of my life. I got hurt. It was a sudden event that made me realize being an athlete was tenuous at best. **If you get hurt, what do you do the next day?**

I knew my injury was the end of it. I had to rethink everything, make some choices about my career, and get more serious about school.

I was studying architecture but wasn't really passionate about it until it was clear that I was not going to be a professional athlete. So I made the choice to explore design on a deeper, more committed level. **I dug in.** I didn't want to just get by. I wanted to absorb it, internalize it, and eventually use it.

Architecture turned out to be a great, well-rounded education and helped me understand the dynamics of creativity, problem-solving, people, and cultures. The design thing started to grow inside of me. After school I continued and got my architect's license.

But then there I was, not quite sure what I was going to do. After all, sports and design are not a common combination. **I ended up coming to Nike at about twenty-eight or twenty-nine as the corporate architect for stores, office remodels, and buildings**. I knew then that job was not the end for me. I just saw it as a way to get into an environment that offered options. It didn't hurt that my track coach at the University of Oregon, Bill Bowerman, was also one of Nike's founders.

It's fortuitous that I ended up here because Nike is all about sports and design and problem solving. **I had to learn a little bit about shoe construction, but it was a relatively seamless transition.** Plus, my father had taught me a lot about competing under pressure, and designing is like being in competition against other companies and other designers. You can't let complicated things mess with your karma. If you're standing at the

HOW WE BOOKED IT

A friend of ours at Nike told us about Tinker. We already knew that he was the master shoe designer, so we called up his assistant Kim and told her about our project. We also mentioned that we were meeting with another exec from Nike who worked with Tinker, Kevin Carroll. That definitely helped because it showed we were already in the door. The assistant told all this to Tinker and, a few weeks later, she got back to us. Tinker said yes.

foul line shooting a free throw, there's a technique to block out distractions so you can focus. Some people here at Nike never got that. They crack under pressure, and actually start to underperform when expectations are high. I never had that problem.

The more experiences you have in life, the easier it is to connect the dots later on. Look at my situation. Architecture is by nature pretty broad. It's both technical and creative and rich in cultural education. To design good buildings, you have to understand people and how they work. Designing shoes and athletic clothing requires the same process.

For example, I had this idea for the Michael Jordan shoe. I'd watched Michael play and observed that he moved like a cat. He was lanky, but when he wanted to he had power and could just launch. To me his movements were catlike. So here at Nike we talked about him being like a black panther. That drove the shoe's design. It had a pawlike sole, black leather, and ticking on the side that looked like a cat's fur.

When I presented the shoe concept to Michael, he started to chuckle, and then he actually got a tear in his eye.

He said, "How did you know that?"

"Know what?" I said.

"That when I was a kid they used to call me the black cat."

So that's the type of connection I'm talking about. You have to spend time getting to know an athlete, his motivations, and his life. Understand his needs and wants. The real fun comes in the end when you make observations that have real meaning. That's the mystical side of designing products.

The larger point here is to broaden your ex-

periences. If you're in design, take some business courses. If you're in business, take a design course. Before you go to law school, travel around the world for a year. Take music lessons. Get on a bus or rent an RV. [Laughs.] And travel around the United States for several weeks.

I'm not designing as much now because I want to teach and mentor. There's something pretty cool about getting to that point. We used to have a sign in my work group that said, "Make yourself useful." At this point in my life—I have three daughters—I've come to understand the importance of helping others. But it took me a while to get here. When you mentor you have to give up that competitive edge. For a while I really wanted to just make a mark for myself. It took some successes until I got to this place in my life.

THE LAST-SECOND SHOT

HOWARD WHITE
Beaverton, Oregon
Vice President and Manager
of the Michael Jordan Brand
Nike
University of Maryland

HOWARD WHITE'S OPEN ROAD MAP

Plays college basketball; accepts that
"getting knocked down is a way of life."

Injured after drafted to NBA; rebounds to become
assistant college coach.

Worried about future, so enters insurance business;
"I didn't know what else to do."

Former teammate recommends Nike job.

Asks Nike founder, "How far could someone
like me go?" Response: "All the way."

Who you are should be defined every day of your life.

$\mathcal{H}oward\ \mathcal{W}hite$ IS TALL, CONFIDENT, AND SPEAKS IN SUCH A DEEP, MESMERIZING VOICE THAT YOU'D SWEAR HE WAS A PREACHER AND NOT A CORPORATE VICE PRESIDENT. WHAT STRUCK US MOST ABOUT HOWARD'S STORY WAS HOW—AFTER HE QUIT PRO BASKETBALL AND WENT INTO BUSINESS—HE CONTINUED TO LIVE BY SIMPLE LESSONS THAT HE LEARNED FROM PLAYING COLLEGE BASKETBALL. THE KID WHO GREW UP IN A POOR CITY NEIGHBORHOOD IS NOW A MAJOR PLAYER AT A $9 BILLION COMPANY AND COUNSELING ATHLETES LIKE MICHAEL JORDAN. AS HOWARD WALKED ACROSS NIKE'S CAMPUS WITH HIS SIGNATURE STRIDE, THERE WASN'T A PERSON WHO DIDN'T SHOUT OUT "YO, H!" BACK AT HIS OFFICE, FLANKED BY SPORTS

PARAPHERNALIA LIKE LANCE ARMSTRONG'S YELLOW JERSEY, HE LEANED BACK IN HIS CHAIR AND LOOKED BACK ON HIS LIFE.

. . . .

My life has been fun, a lot of fun. And I'm not the smartest guy in the world. Hell, I flunked the second grade. What I've learned is not rocket science. It's available to everybody.

Back in college I was playing basketball at the University of Maryland and things just kind of happened. [Pause.] But nothing just <u>happens</u>. You have a huge part in it. How you carry yourself every day. How you represent yourself every day. The passion you show up with every day.

Most people have a gift but don't know what it is. You have to decide what makes you a little different from person X, Y, or Z. I felt that people followed me. That was my gift. When I spoke to people they listened. They paid attention. They wanted more. So you just start building on that.

HOW WE BOOKED iT

Mike: I was a senior in high school when I first saw Howard White speak at a seminar at Pepperdine University. He left an impression on me. Five years later, when we were planning our roadtrip, I asked the chancellor of Pepperdine to recommend people we could meet on the road. He recommended and helped me get in touch with Howard.

People will see greatness in you and you can choose to see it or not. I met a guy in Hawaii who had chiseled a beautiful figure out of a tree. I said, "Man, how did you do that?" He said, "Well, actually the figure was always in the tree. I just let it out. It's not anything special I've done. The figure was there. I only released it from the tree."

In essence, each of us has a wonderful talent inside us, but we need others to help chisel it out, to help fine-tune it, to give us wings. Every step along my way there has been someone who said, "You can do this."

My coach in high school saw me play and he pulled me aside. He said, "Have you ever heard of the Big O—Oscar Robinson?" Who hadn't? Today that's like asking someone if they've ever heard of Michael Jordan. Coach said, "If you listen to everything I tell you, you can be just like the Big O."

I couldn't even play ball. He taught me how to dribble. He taught me how to shoot. He taught me the game of basketball. When I went to college, I was the Big H. I had a big "H" on my uniform.

I accepted that getting knocked down was a way of life. I had a major knee operation in high school and that was before doctors really knew what they were doing. But I played college ball on it. People said, **"How do you play with the knees of a ninety-year-old man?"** I just saw myself playing beyond the rim.

There is going to be pain and there is going to be struggle and there will be times you have to shift your direction. You'll have to take a lot of bullets, but if you stay on that path you can pretty much do what you want to do. Most people just aren't willing to stay on the path. They aren't willing to take the heartache. They aren't willing to get beat on. They aren't willing to get stepped on.

In basketball you are in a world where everyone looks at you. But they see more than just how you play ball. They see how you interact with people, how you help your teammates win.

If you are going to win, it takes a lot more than the effort you give at one particular time. You might hit the last shot that wins the game, yet you've made that shot hundreds of times in private.

It's just the first time others have seen it. That's what the cameras focus on and what everyone jumps up and down about. Most people are seeing it for the first time, but you've done it a million times. **One shot preceded by two million, but that's the one that gets noticed.** While it was luck that you had the last shot to win the game, it was not luck that you shot two million times, every day of your life, waiting for just that opportunity. All of your steps led up to that.

If you're good at ball and if you want to be good at life, you have to show up in life with the same passion that you showed up with to play ball. Not every day will be the most fantastic day of your life. Some days you are going to shoot poorly, some days you're gonna get scored on. Some days you get dunked on, but it is how you rebound from that. All the things that hold people back are learning experiences.

I had another operation my senior year, and I got drafted into the pros. Basketball just wasn't that much fun anymore. My college coach asked me to come on board and help coach. He saw something in me going way back—how I helped, dealt with, and handled people—that made him say I want this person to be a part of this team.

I went forward, but one day I said this coaching stuff is fun but I'm not sure how far it will take me. I talked to Coach about it, and he said if I left I should get into the insurance business, said I could make a lot of money, deal with people. So I went into the insurance business doing estate planning, people's wills, because I didn't know what else to do.

It was all right. Was it fun? No, but it was okay.

While I was in the insurance business, a guy came to me who

happened to be an old teammate. He said there was a great job I would love at Nike.

Here's the interesting part about that. This was the same guy who had been seeing my girlfriend behind my back years ago. He had started messing with drugs and doing the wrong things and I said to myself, "This young man needs help. I need to be around him. I want to help him in his life," and I did. We started getting together, going to dinner, playing tennis. This person was then the one who said, "Here is this wonderful job."

Why do I tell you that story? Most people feel that if a guy had been seeing his girlfriend, they really would not want much to do with him. My approach was to help him. So out of that situation I get this Nike job. Twenty years later I'm a vice president. If I didn't have the fortitude to help him in his dilemma, I would not be here today. No one looks at me and says, "Wow, he helped that guy." All they see now is a vice president of Nike. **Simple lesson: How you treat people is important. I could not have gotten here by myself.**

One day I said to Phil Knight, chief of Nike, how far could someone like me—a guy who flunked the second grade—go in a company like this? Phil looked at his chair and said, "You could go all the way here, if that's what you wanted."

I said, "Well, maybe not, but I like the way you think."

That's it. Simple story, but it's mine.

ROCK STAR

ARIANNE PHILLIPS
Los Angeles, California
Costume Designer and Stylist
San Francisco State University
(never graduated)

ARIANNE PHILLIPS'S OPEN ROAD MAP
↓
Listens to music while recuperating
after college car accident.
↓
Decides to be a stylist on friend's recommendation.
Moves to Manhattan and schmoozes her way into offices
of fashion photographer and editor.
↓
Lands job in fashion television, but prefers
musicians to models.
↓
Quits fashion, waitresses, pals around with young Lenny
Kravitz, and takes random stylist jobs for musicians.
↓
Big break: Styles friend Lenny as he finds fame. Makes a
name for herself designing costumes for movies and
gets new clients like Gwen Stefani and Courtney Love.
↓
Through Courtney Love, meets—and still
works with—Madonna.

I had nothing to lose.

When we met with Arianne AT HER HOUSE
IN HOLLYWOOD, THE FIRST THING SHE SHOWED US WAS A JOURNAL SHE KEPT
WHEN SHE WAS EIGHT YEARS OLD. ITS PAGES WERE FULL OF PENCIL DRAW-
INGS OF CLOTHES—AN EARLY SIGN, SHE SAYS, THAT HER CAREER IS AN HON-
EST EXPRESSION OF WHO SHE IS. HER PATH WASN'T ALWAYS OBVIOUS.
ARIANNE KNEW SHE WANTED TO DO SOMETHING ARTSY BUT STUMBLED INTO
HER CURRENT PROFESSION VIA SOME PRETTY RISKY MANEUVERS. SHE WAS
DRESSED ALL IN BLACK, AND HER HOUSE WAS FULL OF AMAZING OUTFITS AND
COSTUMES THAT SHE DID FOR STARS LIKE MADONNA AND COURTNEY LOVE AND
FOR MOVIES LIKE THE CROW.

I don't remember having a passion. I mean, I didn't grow up saying I wanted to be a costume designer. But I was interested in dressing people up, and my parents had baskets full of costumes they'd get at flea markets. We never had a TV and there weren't a lot of periodicals in the house. My childhood was all about reading literature and going to art museums.

The most important thing I got from my parents—my mother was a writer and my father was a writer and an English teacher—was that I should do what I love. I feel lucky that I was never really pressured to do anything practical or sensible. At the same time, I also knew that I would have to be self-sufficient.

In high school I took beauty school classes for credit. The profession had allure to me because you were encouraged to be an individual. **But I quickly realized that being a hairdresser was not for me.** It was not stimulating enough, although I did get my beauty license and it helped me pay for college.

After a year and a half at school, I got in a bad car accident and had to be flat on my back for six months. So I moved back to my parents' house and holed up in bed, listening to everything from The Clash to John Lennon and reading fashion magazines. One day my friend Rafael Negron called and said he had found the perfect career for me.

"You have to be a stylist," he said.

I asked, "What's a stylist?" He said it was a person who puts clothes together on photo shoots, and he thought I'd be really good at it.

So he and I decided that we were going to New York to be stylists. I figured that I needed something other than a resume. I needed a portfolio. So I had friends take pictures of other friends who were my models. I'd go to the Bargain Barn and buy clothes by the pound, then I'd put the models' outfits together and do their hair and makeup.

I was twenty-one when I got to New York, and I didn't know anyone. A friend of my mom said that I should meet a photographer named Arthur Elgort, who was a friend of a friend. I didn't know who Arthur was, but let me tell you Arthur is one of the most famous fashion photographers ever! At that time he was at his peak.

So I called up Arthur and, instead of saying I was a friend of a friend, I decided to say that I was a direct friend of some person I had never met. I had a lot of chutzpah, which is Yiddish for "nerve." [Laughs.] I got someone on the phone and said I'm a friend of so-and-so and I'm starting in New York as a stylist and I thought Arthur could give me some tips. I called for three days, and they kept saying they'd get back to me. Then one day an assistant called and said Arthur has a lunch break and that I could come in and talk with him.

I put on what I thought was a groovy little outfit. When I got to his studio, I was immediately taken aback. To this day, it is

HOW WE BOOKED IT

Now that we know that Arianne Phillips used cold calls to land her first few jobs in New York, we're not surprised she agreed to meet with us. We first read about her in a magazine and the article published her email address. We sent her a note describing our project, and a few weeks later she called us and chatted for an hour.

rock star

still the most impressive photo studio I have ever seen. Models were everywhere, and there were huge backdrops. I just kept thinking, "I'm a small town girl from Santa Cruz and I can always go back home."

But Arthur was kind and gracious. He looked at my pathetic portfolio and, God bless him, he said as many positive things as he could. A lot of other people would have been harsh. I tried to shrug off the questions he asked me about the person who referred me to him.

Arthur gave me the best advice. **He said I needed to hook up with people from my generation, people like me.** "These are the people you are going to learn and grow with," he said. He also told me that if I wanted to be a stylist, I had to work for Condé Nast. I thought, "Whoever he is, I'm going to work for him."

My boyfriend later told me that Condé Nast was not a man but a publishing company for major fashion magazines, like Vogue and Mademoiselle. So the next day I bought every Condé Nast magazine and called the main number and asked to be put through to the fashion director. I told her assistant that I had recently moved from California, and Arthur Elgort told me that Condé Nast would be a good place for me to start working.

"Fantastic. We'll get right back to you. We would love to meet you. When are you available?" she said.

I'll never forget going to Vogue. I wore the same thrown-together outfit and had the same bad portfolio that I showed Arthur. Here I was in this amazing office when this really chic, beautiful woman walks in and says, "Any friend of Arthur's is a friend of ours."

I realized then that Arthur actually worked with this woman! **I thought I was either going to jail for lying or that I was going to get tortured publicly.** I had stretched the kindness of this man and gotten into hot water. But at some point I figured I was so far into it that I might as well go all the way.

She looked at the portfolio, closed the book, and said she had two things to say. I figured she was going to call security. I was dead.

So she says, "Which do you want first, the good thing or the bad?"

"The bad thing," I say.

She said, "I don't think you're right for <u>Vogue</u>." I'm like "No shit." "But I think you're perfect for <u>Mademoiselle</u>."

I was shocked. She sent me to the head of personnel and told her that I was a friend of Arthur's. I filled out an application and just went for it. She said they didn't have any jobs, but to call every week until something opened.

Four days later I got a phone call from a woman who said she was recommended to me by Condé Nast's personnel department. She needed interns for a television show for the Lifetime Network. The job didn't pay, but it was employment and I was young enough that I didn't mind; you have to start somewhere and build your resume. I just wanted that foot in the right door.

After ten episodes, the show didn't get renewed, but the stylist on the show recommended five other stylists that I should call. He said I could use his name. So I called them up and ended up working for a woman who had been a big editor at a fashion magazine and now did advertising campaigns. I was her fourth assistant and got to work with top models. She wasn't the best teacher, and it wasn't a lot of fun, and I realized that while I liked fashion I didn't think I could handle a steady diet of it. A lot of fashion is establishment, and I wasn't into that. I wanted to do edgier work. I assisted her for two months, realized it was not for me, and then got a waitressing job.

I never did finish college. My parents were really disappointed, but I was trying to make my way. I was just not sure what my way was. It unfolded itself.

I decided to go into rock 'n' roll where there were people I had more in common with. There is something about working with musicians where the product is music. I could get behind that more than a facial cleanser or a pair of jeans.

A magical thing happened. A mutual friend introduced me to Lenny Kravitz. He was a poor, starving musician who was playing drums and no one had ever heard of him. We became fast friends and hung out all the time. He'd talk about making his record, and I'd say I was going to be his stylist! Then he went off to do his thing in L.A. and I continued trying to carve out my niche in New York.

My portfolio was getting better, and I started to get names of people at record companies. It was really hard to pick up the phone and convince people that meeting me would be worth fifteen minutes of their time. There was a lot of rejection, but I had nothing to lose. I just kept persevering.

I did small jobs, like ironing Peter Gabriel's suit or, when Paul Young was in town doing <u>Saturday Night Live</u>, finding him a black jacket, little things like that.

I did my first music video, Buster Poindexter's "Hot Hot Hot," in the 1980s. Meanwhile, Lenny Kravitz and I kept in touch. He moved back to New York to work on his record. There were a lot of exciting things happening, and the work I did with him was my first break in terms of people taking notice of me.

I did more and more with Lenny. In the beginning we were really ridiculed. Slowly the tide turned and people sought me out. The next step was to work on a movie, and I made a film with some film students in New York. Once again, I taught myself.

When I moved back to L.A., I befriended Brandon Lee, who recommended me for his new movie The Crow. I got the job and it was one of the most creative environments I'd ever been in, but it was also the worst experience of my life because Brandon died during filming. I've never been able to really celebrate that movie. It was a weird way to start in the film business, but it gave me momentum. I got more credibility after I did The People vs. Larry Flynt, when I worked with Courtney Love. She eventually introduced me to Madonna, and that brought me back into the fashion and music world.

Six or seven years ago I saw a magazine headline that said, "Learn how to stop hating your job." It had never occurred to me that you could.

THE ACCIDENTAL LAWYER

EDWARD MASRY
Westlake Village, California
Environmental Attorney, Masry & Vititoe
Mayor
Attended several
colleges but holds no
undergrad degree
Loyola Law School

ED MASRY'S OPEN ROAD MAP

Parties and plays sports in junior college.

Joins the navy, then the army, ships to France.

Attends various colleges and serendipitously takes law school admission exam; gets into law school without college degree but graduates with honors.

A trial lawyer for thirty years until a heart attack curtails his work.

Stumbles into and wins lawsuit with help of employee Erin Brockovich.

Continues to practice law; gets into politics and is elected city mayor.

Find out what's going on in the world.

Ed Masry IS THE CROTCHETY LAWYER PORTRAYED BY ALBERT FINNEY IN THE OSCAR-WINNING MOVIE <u>ERIN BROCKOVICH</u>. THE FILM IS ABOUT A SASSY, SMART, SINGLE MOM (PLAYED BY JULIA ROBERTS) WHO GETS A JOB IN A LAW OFFICE, STUMBLES ACROSS SOME QUESTIONABLE FILES, AND CONVINCES THE HEAD OF THE FIRM, ED, TO PURSUE A COSTLY LAWSUIT AGAINST A HUGE UTILITY COMPANY, PG&E. PLAINTIFFS ACCUSED THE COMPANY OF CONTAMINATING WATER IN HINKLEY, CALIFORNIA, AND CAUSING DOZENS OF RESIDENTS TO GET SICK. PG&E EVENTUALLY SETTLED OUT OF COURT AND PAID THE PLAINTIFFS ABOUT $333 MILLION. A CHUNK OF THAT WENT TO MASRY'S LAW FIRM AS HIS CONTINGENCY FEE. HE MET WITH US IN HIS BEAU-

TIFUL CORNER OFFICE OVERLOOKING THE MOUNTAINS. HE WASN'T WEARING
SHOES, JUST BLACK SOCKS.

···

I've always been concerned about someone picking on somebody else. I guess that's because I grew up very poor. I actually lived in a tent for three years. My parents had a small bungalow and there was never really room for me, so my dad bought a tent where I slept on the ground. It was a big deal when he finally bought me a bed.

We worked on a farm, woke up with the roosters, and went to work in the dark. In high school I ran track, did cross-country, and played football. At seventeen I graduated and tried to get into the Marines, but they wouldn't have me unless my parents signed, and they wouldn't. So there I was, cleaning out my high school locker when the coach for the local junior college came over and offered me a scholarship. It was five dollars a week and I had to cut the grass. I entered Valley College in February 1950. Just going to junior college was a big deal for my parents. I have a brother and sister who never got out of high school, and another sister who graduated but never went to college. Valley Junior College was a great party school. **I was always a party freak** but never really a smoker or a doper or a heavy drinker. I guess that's because my parents, who are from Syria and France, said we could drink and smoke when we were kids. I could have a glass of wine at six years old if I wanted.

In college I ran track, played football, got active in a fraternity, became student body president, and headed a bunch of clubs. I ended up joining the Navy Reserve, and when the Korean War started, I joined the army. In those days it was a very patriotic thing to do. They shipped me to France instead of Korea because I spoke both Arabic and French fluently. When I got to France in 1952, there was a lot of dope, particularly around Paris. None of the guys around me gave a damn about dope. It was no big deal.

After the service I wanted to be a doctor because I thought they made good money. But I failed zoology—it was a boring class. I went to Santa Barbara College for one semester, fooled around, and had less than a C average. I was failing out, so I quickly moved to the University of California before my grades could catch up with me. [Laughs.]

One day I was being driven to a party, and the guy who was driving was also taking the Loyola Law School admission test. I was going to wait for him, but it turned out that I could take the exam for free because I was a veteran, so I did. A month later the dean called me and said I had been admitted. I had scored phenomenally high on the test and they let me in.

When I started law school, I was the only one without a

HOW WE BOOKED IT

Mike: I guessed that the name of Ed's law firm in the movie _Erin Brockovich_ was the real name of his law firm. It turned out to be a good hunch. I searched for Masry & Vititoe on Google and found the firm's Web page, called the main number, and, as usual, got transferred to the public relations department. It was obvious that the firm was inundated with interview requests after the movie, and the PR rep made us submit a proposal and a letter explaining ourselves. After we sent in our stuff, I called once a week for about four months! Each time the rep was very brisk. One day she softened up a bit (maybe she was just sick of me calling) and scheduled our meeting with Ed. Truth be told, we think it helped our cause that we didn't want to speak with Erin Brockovich, who got most of the calls. Instead, we wanted her less sexy counterpart.

bachelor's degree. They didn't think I'd make it, but I graduated with honors.

Until my second year in law school, it never occurred to me what I was going to do. **Up to that point, my life had been totally random. I had no direction.** Then I became editor of a newspaper, and became what you might call a "radical."

About six months after law school, I went out on my own, and over the years tried about every type of case I could. I was a trial lawyer for thirty years. In 1991 I was defending a $1.5 billion money laundering case when I had a heart attack in court. They took a two-week recess, and when the trial was finally over I promised my wife that I would never go back to the courtroom.

Then I stumbled onto Hinkley. The movie is basically true. I thought it kind of helped trial lawyers because it showed the American people that contingency lawyers risk a lot. We have to put our money where our mouths are.

Afterward I became heavily involved in environmental law and supervising this law office. I wasn't remotely interested in politics, and then one day my wife and I watched a city hall meeting on television. It showed a group of people blasting this woman who was running for office. My wife and I said, "This is B.S.," and we called her up and donated $50,000 to her campaign. Soon, her opposition sent two mailers calling me a convicted felon, a money launderer, a drug pusher. All of a sudden I was on the front pages.

STUDENT FEEDBACK

Jill, a senior majoring in advertising, joined us on our meeting with Ed: 'Sometimes I feel inadequate because I don't yet know what to do with my life. The fear of getting stuck on a path that I don't enjoy makes me hesitate to make any decisions. It was reassuring to hear Ed talk about changing his direction in life. He never intended to go to law school, but look where he is now. He helped me realize that as long as I move in some direction that I enjoy at that time, it's okay. I can always change."

It was ridiculous. The next thing you know, every environmentalist was knocking on my door asking for help.

In 2000, I decided that I didn't like all the real estate development that was going on around here, so I ran for city council and was elected. Now I assume I'll be voted in as mayor of Thousand Oaks tomorrow night. It's kind of frightening. I was jailed five times while I was an attorney, and now I'm probably going to be the mayor. [Laughs.] It's kind of scary when you think about it.

I'm sixty-nine now and having a good time. I'm on kidney dialysis. I go in three days a week for four hours and fifteen minutes, starting at 4:30 A.M. But I'm doing fine. I feel great, and I enjoy the law, I enjoy what we do here. **We do a lot of good and we make a lot of money**. I try to do what I can to make things right. We now have suits filed against every automobile dealer in California. It's the biggest class-action suit in the state. I look at things and say, "This is right, this isn't." So I do the little bit I can to try and make it right.

I got here by a series of coincidences. My advice? Don't do what I did. Study and find out what's going on in the world.

THE REAL JERRY MAGUIRE

LEIGH STEINBERG
Newport Beach, California
Lawyer and Sports Agent
President, Assante Enterprises
University of California, Berkeley

LEIGH STEINBERG'S OPEN ROAD MAP

Thrives in college at Berkeley during tumultuous 1960s.

↓

Pursues plan to be a "lawyer for the downtrodden."

↓

Jumps in Egypt's Nile and contracts disease;
laid up for months.

↓

While recuperating, represents a college friend
and football player turning pro;
negotiates player's huge contract.

↓

Realizes "athletes are the new celebrities";
embraces life as agent who sculpts athletes
as charitable role models.

↓

Thrives with top clients; adjusts as industry shifts
to "content supply."

Twenty-six years ago there were no sports agents.

Remember the movie JERRY MAGUIRE, STARRING
TOM CRUISE? LEIGH STEINBERG WAS THE INSPIRATION FOR THE LEAD CHAR-
ACTER—THE SPORTS AGENT WITH A HEART. SURPRISINGLY, LEIGH FOUND HIS
ROAD NOT BECAUSE HE LOVED SPORTS BUT BECAUSE HE WANTED TO BE A
LAWYER AND WANTED TO DO GOOD IN THE WORLD. TODAY HIS FIRM REPRE-
SENTS ABOUT 150 ATHLETES, INCLUDING FOOTBALL PLAYERS RICKY WILLIAMS
OF THE MIAMI DOLPHINS AND TROY AIKMAN, A BROADCASTER AND FORMER
DALLAS COWBOYS PLAYER. WE MET LEIGH IN HIS POSH CORNER OFFICE OVER-
LOOKING NEWPORT BEACH, CALIFORNIA. IT'S CRAMMED WITH PHO-
TOGRAPHS AND SPORTS MEMORABILIA LIKE AUTOGRAPHED FOOTBALLS AND

HELMETS. HE MAY NOT BE TOM CRUISE, BUT HE'S DEFINITELY SHOWN HIS CLIENTS THE MONEY.

I't's okay to have uncertainty.

I was in Berkeley in 1967 and 1968, probably the most tumultuous time on college campuses. The Vietnam War was going on. It was the summer of love, long hair, tie-dye clothes, the Beatles, marijuana, and radical politics. Berkeley was the center of it all. It's hard to imagine a time when every philosophy was more under fire. I loved it. It was totally exciting and very heady. I ended up being student body president.

Having said all that, I always knew I wanted to be a lawyer. I watched Perry Mason as a kid and viewed myself as this great lawyer for the downtrodden. I knew I wanted to make a difference in the world.

My father brought us up to believe that we shouldn't look to other people to deal with injustice or oppression. My brothers and I had to change it. **We were essentially brought up to be activists**. It wasn't for us to sit on the sidelines, so I never really had any ambivalence about what I was going to do. Plus, I loved the concept of being at trial, so I thought I'd work for the district attorney.

I went to law school straight from college. After graduation I went on a tour of the world and when I was in Egypt I jumped in the Nile River. Let's just say the Nile was not that pristine [laughs], and I contracted a tropical disease. I was put in a hospital in London and dropped about 60 pounds. I was in no condition to practice law, so I hung out for about two years recuperating.

In 1975 I got a call from a football player at Berkeley, Steve Bartkowski, who I'd met when I was a dorm counselor during law school. That year, Steve was the very first player picked in the National Football League draft, and he asked me to represent him. **Although I'd never practiced law, my client was the very first pick in the NFL draft!** The bidding went back and forth. We eventually negotiated the largest rookie contract in the history of football.

After negotiating the contract, Steve and I arrived at the Atlanta airport the night before the signing. We got off the plane and the scene was like a movie premiere. There were lights flashing, people were pressed up against a police line, and the first thing we heard was, "We interrupt The Johnny Carson Show to bring you a special news bulletin. Steve Bartkowski and his attorney Leigh Steinberg have just arrived at the airport. We switch you live for an in-depth interview."

Athletes had become the new celebrities. I saw the tremendous idol worship and made up my mind to

HOW WE BOOKED IT

The idealistic sports agent portrayed in the movie Jerry Maguire was trapped in a professional box and broke out to pursue his own road. Naturally we wanted to meet the person on whom the character was based. We were lucky because one of our friends knew Leigh's assistant, so we called her up and gave her our pitch. Being referred by a mutual friend definitely helped. She asked us to fax over a one-page explanation, and eventually Leigh agreed to sit down with us.

work with athletes, and I saw the power they could have as role models.

That was twenty-six years ago, when there was no field of so-called sports agents. Athletes had no guaranteed right of representation, and quite often they were exploited. A couple years later, players finally had the right to be represented.

The perception of sports agents has never been all that positive because athletes' pay is directly related to ticket prices. Fans resent the high salaries. My function is not just economic. It's to enhance the most positive qualities of a young man. To build his self-respect, help him live in a family, be part of a community, and to help him plan for a second career. I want athletes to be role models. Look at Warren Moon, the client I've worked with the longest. He went back to his high school, junior college, and university and started a scholarship fund to help students pay for college.

Anyone considering working in the sports industry should realize how quickly the field can change. In the time I've been in this business, it's gone from just negotiating sports contracts to having dozens of ancillary revenue opportunities. I've had to adjust from simply negotiating a percentage of a client's contract to looking at my clients as potential content for television, radio, video games, the Internet. My life has changed dramatically.

STUDENT FEEDBACK

Jake was a junior studying economics when he came with us to visit Leigh. Although Jake wasn't sure what to do after college, he gleaned some guidance.

"Leigh never seemed to be all about money even though it's obvious he's been successful. That was really cool. You have to find something you love to do and be around people you enjoy, not just what builds your savings account."

That said, what's really necessary is to attain the basic skills. I tell people who want to go into the sports field to study business. Athletes don't want a person who can tell them the batting average for the 1939 World Series. They want people who can bring them business, legal, and financial skills. The basic skills are most important.

The contracts that I negotiate are not the ultimate measure of my success. Have I made a difference in the lives of young men? Have the charitable programs I set up made a difference in the world? Anyone trying to make the world better knows you have to work at it. It's like having a list of fifty things to do and saying, "I'll never get these things done!" The hell with that. You have to do the first thing, then the second and the third and, eventually, you start to make a dent.

ABSOLUTE INTUITION

LAURIE COOTS
Los Angeles, California
TBWA/Chiat/Day
Chief Marketing Officer Worldwide
Colorado State University

LAURIE COOTS'S OPEN ROAD MAP

Off to veterinary school to live out childhood dream.

Struggles with a change of heart,
but drops out despite pressure.

Rides horses, enters hotel business, starts a family.

Hungry to "make an impact," demotes herself and
takes job as secretary for progressive ad agency.

Over eighteen years, reinvents her role within agency,
rising through ranks.

Just because you're competent at something doesn't mean it will fuel your passion.

TBWA/Chiat/Day's CLIENTS IN-
CLUDE ABSOLUT VODKA, NISSAN, AND APPLE COMPUTER. ITS FUNKY OFFICE
IN PLAYA DEL REY, CALIFORNIA, LOOKS MORE LIKE AN ART MUSEUM THAN A
CORPORATE BUILDING. THE MIDDLE SECTION OF ITS FAÇADE IS DESIGNED TO
LOOK LIKE A GIANT PAIR OF BINOCULARS. INSIDE, IT'S OPEN AND COLOR-
FUL. THERE'S A BAR, A HUGE BASKETBALL COURT, AND A SECTION WITH
TREES AND FOLIAGE DUBBED CENTRAL PARK. THAT'S WHERE WE SAT DOWN
WITH LAURIE AND TALKED. AFTER THE INTERVIEW WE WERE THE "GUEST
SPEAKERS" AT THE AGENCY'S WEEKLY KEG PARTY, WHICH WAS HELD ON THE
HIP INDOOR BASKETBALL COURT.

As a kid I was going to be a veterinarian because I rode horses competitively and I loved science. I also loved taking things apart and putting them back together. But after a couple of years in veterinary school, I realized it wasn't for me. I was good at it—I even liked surgery—but it didn't make me happy.

So I dropped out.

Talk about traumatic! For ten years I was going to be a veterinarian! Just admitting to myself that I didn't want to do it took a year. But once you finally say, "Okay, this is not it," you have to believe that it's the right decision. Yes, there was a lot of pressure not to quit. I was one of two women who were accepted to the school and it was an honor to be there. People challenged me on it. They said I had taken someone's place. And I think my dad was a little freaked that I wasn't going to have this fabulous degree to hang on my wall; he thought I was destined to live a life of poverty. [Laughs.] But I just wouldn't have been happy. You have to trust your gut. **Sometimes being clear about what you don't want is almost as important as being clear about what you do want.**

Leaving vet school was the first "ah-ha" moment in my life because my assumption had always been that if you're good at something it will automatically make you happy. But just because you're competent at something doesn't necessarily mean it will fuel your passion.

I left school and rode horses for a few years. I also spent time in the hotel business, but when you get promoted they want you to move like 3,000 miles away. But by then I'd gotten married and had a baby, and I realized that the hotel industry wasn't going to work out for me.

Meanwhile, I had met people from Chiat/Day who had talked about the company's great attitude. I didn't know anything about advertising, but I inquired about a job. For a while they didn't have anything but, finally, a secretarial position for the Apple Computer account opened. **So I bit the bullet and started completely over as a secretary**. It was tough, let me tell you. I went from having a pretty good life as a marketing director for Hilton to saving up money for panty hose. [Laughs.]

When I interviewed for the Apple account, they asked me if I knew computers. I lied and said yes. So, yes, I kind of bullshitted my way in, but once there I was really committed to making sure that everyone felt that they hadn't made a mistake by hiring me.

Where did I get the courage? I was looking for a place where I could make a big impact. That was one of the problems I had

with medicine: It would have taken me too long to become good enough to be a world-changing surgeon. At Chiat/Day, I thought, "Where can I be a part of a place or a group of people who believe they can change the world every day?" That's what I wanted to sign up for. I didn't know where I was going to go, but I knew that I'd be a better person for having done it.

I never intended to stay for eighteen years. But in that period I've reinvented myself six or seven times. I've been a secretary, I've helped change the way we pitch new business, I've run human resources for North America, and in 1994 I was in charge of creating Chiat/Day's first virtual office environment, where we took away everybody's desk!

Now I have a son who's a sophomore in college. He's so creative, but I worry about his last two years of school. A lot of juniors and seniors don't read the newspaper every day. They get myopic. They are out of touch with the world, and when you do that you lose touch with your intuition. **A lot of students coming out of school have had the intuition just beaten out of them**. To follow your bliss you must know what your bliss is, and the only way to know that is by trying new things and having different life experiences. If you're too directed, you run the risk of eliminating choices before you ever see them. That's sad to me.

DECODE YOUR ROAD

J. CRAIG VENTER, PH.D.
Rockville, Maryland
Scientist, Human Genome Decoder
University of California, San Diego

CRAIG VENTER'S OPEN ROAD MAP

Barely graduates high school, gets D in physics;
works at Sears until drafted.

Joins medical corps and ships to Vietnam.

After Vietnam, trains as a scientist and gets Ph.D.

Heads large lab at National Institutes of Health;
quits out of frustration with bureaucracy.

Despite criticism, starts own organization
for unique genetic research.

Venture money supports his team that
decodes human genome.

If I let everyone else influence what we were doing, then the human genome wouldn't be sequenced now.

Craig Venter LED A TEAM OF PEOPLE—AND BUILT A CADRE OF COMPUTERS—THAT DECODED THE SEQUENCE OF THE HUMAN GENOME IN 2000. IT WAS A TASK HE HAD ATTEMPTED FOR YEARS WHILE WORKING AT THE NATIONAL INSTITUTES OF HEALTH. BUT HE GOT FRUSTRATED WITH THE GOVERNMENT'S SLOW, LINEAR PROCEDURES AND QUIT TO FOUND THE INSTITUTE FOR GENOMIC RESEARCH, A NOT-FOR-PROFIT ORGANIZATION. IN 1998 HE STARTED A FOR-PROFIT COMPANY, CELERA GENOMICS. IT WAS THERE THAT DR. VENTER'S PLAN SUCCEEDED AND HIS DISCOVERY MADE HEADLINES. HIS MOST INFLUENTIAL SELF-DISCOVERY, HOWEVER, CAME WHEN HE GOT OUT OF THE MILITARY. AFTER WATCHING OTHERS RISK THEIR LIVES IN WAR, HE RE-

ALIZED THAT NOT TO RISK ONE'S LIFE EMOTIONALLY AND SPIRITUALLY—OR, IN OTHER WORDS, NOT TO FOLLOW ONE'S OPEN ROAD—IS TANTAMOUNT TO FAILURE.

. . . .

I had a rebellious youth. School was boring, so I never paid much attention. It was unrewarding, and in high school I only took two science classes, got a D in physics, and came within half a grade of graduating. I left home at seventeen.

To support myself I worked as a night clerk at Sears, putting labels on things, so I could surf during the day. I also worked as a lifeguard and as a baggage handler. Menial labor is very motivating. It convinces you that there has to be better stuff to do in life. Working at Sears definitely helped me figure out what I <u>didn't</u> want to do. [Laughs.] I finally decided I should go to school, so I started at a junior college in Southern California.

In 1965 I got drafted and was told to report to the Army, but my parents, who were in the Marines, told me that the Marines were cooler than the Army. But as a competitive swimmer, I was ultimately recruited to join the Navy swimming team. All I had to do was go through boot camp. My Navy uniform would be a Speedo.

HOW WE BOOKED IT

Mike: While I studied biology in college, I was constantly reading about Dr. Venter's race with the government to decode the human genome. He was one of the first people I cold called to interview for the roadtrip. I visited Celera's Web site, called directory assistance in Rockville, Maryland, and was eventually transferred to not one but four assistants who asked for a proposal. Once Craig said yes, it took another month to get on his calendar. It was worth the effort. The stuff he told us in person was more inspiring than anything I'd read in my college textbooks.

About two-thirds of the way through boot camp, President Johnson escalated the war in Vietnam and cancelled all military sports teams. I had to find a new field. Because I wanted to be able to get a job after the military, I went into the medical corps.

I loved it. I got exposure to things I knew nothing about, and I got more training each day than most physicians get in a year. In fact, within a year I was running one of the biggest disease wards in the military, and I was teaching interns how to do basic procedures. I did liver biopsies, spinal taps—I discovered my skills and realized that I was good at tasks requiring hand-eye coordination.

Eventually I was sent to DeNang, in Vietnam, where I worked—and surfed—for a year. Yes, people really did surf in Vietnam. **It was some of the wildest surfing I've ever done**, and it wasn't very safe because of sharks and poisonous sea snakes.

Meanwhile, at the hospital, I worked twelve-hour shifts. That's where I really learned about medicine and realized that knowledge was power. The right knowledge can save people's lives. When I got out of the military I was twenty-two and very motivated to go back to school. I was interested in practicing Third World medicine, so I went to a junior college for a year and a half and then transferred to the University of California at San Diego. I worked with a famous researcher and he gave me my own lab. It was then that I decided to go into science instead of medicine.

I didn't start to excel until I got to a point where my unique mental capacities could really make a difference. I'm a quick learner but not through memorization, and the United States' education system is geared toward memorization and regurgitation. Some people excelled at that, but I didn't. I think part of my success came because I had to work harder to understand concepts versus just memorizing stuff. That type of conceptual thinking is perfect for the field I'm in, where we try to come up with new approaches and ideas.

It's only when you get into the higher end of science that it counts to have a good imagination. It's actually very easy to make new discoveries and uncover things that all the people with great memorization skills can't understand. It's not hard to do! **I actually make discoveries by ignoring what other people have done**.

Another big lesson I learned in Vietnam was to take risks, and I took what some people saw as unbelievable risks. For example, I had a big government job with a huge budget and guaranteed lifetime employment, but I couldn't take ideas to the next stage because of the bureaucracy. So I gave up the job to start the Institute for Genomic Research.

That was risky, and not something I advise anybody to do. If you leave a stable job and fail at something else, you can't always get that first job back again. There are knowledge risks and there are blind risks. Swimming in the midst of sea snakes was a blind risk, and I've done foolish things like that which I wouldn't recommend anyone repeat. **Still, taking risks is the only way to advance**.

Most people thought what I did at Celera was very foolish. Senior scientists were saying our approach wouldn't work. But I've never been influenced much by other people's comments. If I

FOURTEEN-HOUR U-TURN

We spent a year trying to book a meeting with Craig Venter, but it wasn't until we were on the road that he gave us a date. Unfortunately, it was a Friday at 9:00 A.M., and we had already scheduled meetings in New York the day before and the day after that. But there was no way we could cancel the man who decoded the human genome. We couldn't leave Manhattan until 10:30 P.M. the night before, and it was a six-hour trip to Washington! We drove all night, pulled into Celera's parking lot at 4:30 A.M., and got a few hours of sleep. After the interview we made a U-turn and headed back to Manhattan for our interview with Jehane Noujaim.

let everyone else influence what we were doing, the human genome wouldn't be sequenced now.

Ask yourself what you want to accomplish in life, pick a goal, and decide what you will contribute to make society a better place. There are some real challenges facing us. **You can either be part of the problem, or part of the solution**.

Note: Not long after we met with Craig Venter, he left Celera Genomics. In August 2002 he announced plans to build a large, not-for-profit genome sequencing center that would decrease the time required to decode people's DNA.

decode your road

PROFILES FROM THE MOVEMENT

INTRODUCTION

When we got home from our first road trip, the experiences and inspiration we gathered while on the road had fueled us to make something more of Roadtrip Nation. It wasn't a far stretch to assume that others were in similar situations to what we were experiencing—confused about the next step and feeling heightened levels of pressure to conform.

In addition to reading a book, or watching a documentary, we could feel that others needed to experience the road—first hand. They needed to get out there and absorb all that inspiration based on what *their* passions, interests, and beliefs were. We began to realize that the best thing we could do to help others *find* their open road was to actually help them *hit* the road.

Knowing that financing was probably the first barrier (we learned this the hard way) we began to raise money from organizations to fund other trips. With these resources, Roadtrip Nation started and currently runs two programs: the first, "Behind the Wheel," provides funding to hit the road in one of three Roadtrip Nation green RVs. The second program, "Roadtrip Nation Grants" offers grants to hit the road in your own vehicle.

If you've found a certain degree of inspiration and clarity from this book so far, hitting the road takes that impact to an exponentially higher level.

What you'll find in this next section of the book are the reflections and interviews from others who have hit the road, and four new profiles that are included in a PBS series we've put together. Perhaps you'll get a glimpse of what your own trip could be like. Then, if you feel that calling inside you to get out there and encounter the road for yourself, the last section of this book, "Do it Yourself," is there to help you make it happen.

Maybe we can even help with the funds through one of our programs, if that's an issue, as we're assuming it is. "Behind the Wheel" is run through a limited number of college career centers, but "Roadtrip Nation Grants" are open to everyone. Applications are online at the Roadtrip Nation Web site (www.roadtripnation.com), and the deadline is rolling. Whatever the case, we hope that the first-hand reflections and experiences in this section stimulate you to seriously consider *mobilizing* the inspiration you've gleaned from this book so far.

The road is open to everyone. It sits there waiting—and what it offers is a significant reflection point that one day you'll look back on and say; "I can't imagine what my life would have been like if I had not given it a go."

FLYING HIGH

DAVID NEELEMAN'S OPEN ROAD MAP

↓

Grows up with learning disability; did "very poorly on standardized tests."

↓

"Obligatorily" goes to college, but "doesn't do very well."

↓

Starts first business and then drops out of college.

↓

Business fails, but still needs to support family; "those were lean times."

↓

Starts second business, Morris Air, the first airline to offer electronic ticketing.

↓

Sells the innovative airline to Southwest and was "set for life" at age thirty-two.

↓

Fired from Southwest after six months; "it devastated me."

↓

Launches JetBlue in 2000; boasts most profitable first year in airline history.

↓

Listed as one of _Time_ magazines 100 Most Influential People, between bin Laden and the pope.

DAVID NEELEMAN
Salt Lake City Area, Utah
CEO of JetBlue Airways
Attended University of Utah,
but dropped out

My definition of success is *mattering*.

Born with ATTENTION DEFICIT DISORDER (ADD), DAVID STRUG-
GLED THROUGH SCHOOL. HE SLOWLY CAME TO RECOGNIZE THAT HIS DISEASE WAS
ACTUALLY AN ASSET: ONE CHARACTERISTIC OF ADD IS THE ABILITY TO FOCUS
ON ONE CENTRAL INTEREST, DRIVING HIM TO THINK UP IDEAS THAT OTHERS
DON'T. BECAUSE OF THIS HE REFUSES TO TAKE MEDICATION FOR FEAR OF BE-
ING ROBBED OF HIS CREATIVITY. HE'S A FATHER OF NINE AND STILL FINDS THE
TIME TO WORK AS A FLIGHT ATTENDANT ON HIS AIRLINE EACH MONTH. DESPITE
HIS ENORMOUS SUCCESS, HE DONATES HIS ENTIRE $200,000 SALARY TO CHAR-
ITY EACH YEAR. AMIDST THE RECENT CORPORATE SCANDALS THAT HAVE BEEN
PLAGUING OUR COUNTRY, IT WAS REFRESHING TO INTERVIEW A CEO PASSION-
ATE ABOUT BUILDING AN ORGANIZATION, NOT JUST MAKING MONEY.

It has been well publicized that I have a learning disability. I had a hard time focusing and I did very poorly on standardized tests.

My ACT score was so low in English that my teacher told me that if I would have picked C for every answer, I would have done better . . . maybe 30% better. For someone who was in my position then to get to where I am today I had to stay positive, not give up, and basically keep looking at the bright side of life.

I believe that if people have a good attitude and look at how to make things better, as opposed to criticizing things, they will be hugely successful.

When I was nine years old I started working in my grandpa's grocery store. I spent time with customers and I learned the pricing side of the business. I felt like I had an aptitude and a passion for business, but I didn't know exactly what I was going to do with it. I figured if I got an accounting degree then I could do anything—I could get security or something. Can you imagine me being an accountant? [laughs].

I obligatorily went to college, but didn't do very well so I ended up leaving to go on a church mission to Brazil, where I spent two years working among the poorest of the poor.

After that, I came back and returned to school. I still didn't like it, but I did a lot better because I was learning how to channel and focus. I was trying to do something in business, but it really worried me because I hadn't read that much in my life and it was hard for me to write. As it turned out, I had gifts and talents that other people didn't have and it served me well.

Finally, I had an opportunity to start my own business in the travel area and **I dropped out of college.** I took a leap of faith because it was something that I felt strongly about. When I first dropped out of college, my parents were very disappointed. They really wanted their son to be a college graduate.

That business ended up failing, but I learned from it. **Those were lean times.** I had two kids, house payments, car payments, and no job. I was back at the grocery store and deciding whether or not to go back to school. Adversity will come your way. There's no doubt about it. There's not a person on the planet that has not experienced some form of failure in their life—and

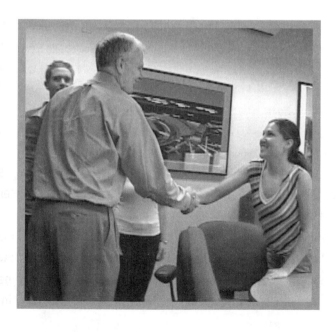

f
l
y
i
n
g

h
i
g
h

I believe it's not about what happens to you in life, it's how you react, bounce back, and learn from the experience.

That's what I did when I failed in my first business venture. The reason it failed is because I was undercapitalized. And I realized with my next company that I should never be undercapitalized. So I started another business, Morris Air. That was very successful. I sold it to Southwest Airlines when I was thirty-two and was set for life.

I can remember when I was twenty-eight years old and I paid off my house. I wasn't very old and I went to the local banker, where my family had always done business. My father didn't have a lot of money and his banker was always covering bounced checks for him. When one of his kids walked in and paid off his house, it was like "Whoa, what is going on here?" The bank actually called my company and said they thought I had embezzled money since no Neeleman could have made that kind of money.

I then began to work for Southwest Airlines, but I got fired after six months. I didn't like working in the environment of a big company where I had to go through so many channels and protocols. It's good to be able to walk down the halls and into someone's office and say "Hey, have we thought about doing this?" without having an appointment or having to write a memo about it. Being fired from Southwest Airlines devastated me. It was my dream job, everything about them made me excited. I got in there with enthusiasm and asked if they could do things a little differently and I was asked to leave.

At that point I could have gone and not done anything with the rest of my life—I already had money and kids—but I wanted to start something better than Southwest. I wanted to take that negative experience, learn from it, and parlay it into something better—which is what I did with JetBlue.

Again I learned that **it's not about what happens to you in life. It's how you react to it,** what you learn from those experiences.

But that's easier said than done. It's difficult when you are in the throes of it to actually do it. As I look back on my negative experiences—in hindsight, I didn't actually stop and say "What have I learned from my experiences?" I was just someone who didn't want to fail. When I left Southwest, I had this fire in my gut to create another airline.

I had a five-year non-compete clause in my contract that had four and a half years left on it. At that point I said, "That will give me four and a half years to build the best airline." I started building JetBlue from that minute.

Internally you have to tell yourself "I'm not going to let them get me down. I'm going to bounce back and I'm going to bounce back further and harder than I have in the past. And I'm going to learn from this experience."

I have a disdain for people who feel that they are better than others. When you get money, there is this temptation to not associate with your customers or employees. You get chauffeurs and you go with the luxuries of life. That's not in me. That's not who I am.

One of the things I realized during the time I sold my business, went to work at Southwest, was fired, and had to give all the money back in order to start JetBlue, was that money wasn't the most important thing to me. It was the building of the business—the chase—it was positively influencing the lives of others by building a better company.

That was a really good lesson to learn at thirty-two years

old—to say to myself "You don't need money, it's more about helping others."

That's why I have a $200,000 salary that I donate to a JetBlue member crisis fund. As our crew members put in a dollar, I put in a dollar and our president also puts in a dollar. Last year we raised $800,000 that we awarded to our crew members for catastrophic need situations like hurricanes.

It's important to do things for others. When I was on my mission in Brazil, the leader of that mission told me something that impacted me greatly. He said, "You have spent the past two years losing yourself in the service of others and have found great happiness in doing it. Now you are going to go home and do things for yourself—it's all going to be about you. Until you find a way to service others in life, you will never find your full measure of happiness."

I have always taken that to heart. We have 8,500 people at JetBlue, and the vast majority will tell you that this is the best job that they have ever had. That is because I want to be a leader who people can respect and follow, not a leader who is trying to rape and pillage the company for as much money as they can get. I can be this kind of a leader because I learned that money doesn't mean that much to me.

One time a CEO of a very successful company came to me. He wanted to become a better CEO. He spent $10,000 to go to a well-known educational institution for a weekend to improve his skills. What he learned during that retreat was that if his company was plucked from the face of the earth and his customers came to do business with him only to find it gone, would they care?

Did his company <u>matter</u> to his customers and his employees? Would his employees say "That guy didn't give me any health benefits" and/or "he didn't pay me well"? He was asked to come up with a company that mattered to him, and the first company that came to mind was JetBlue. He said, "I fly JetBlue back and forth to Florida every week. You matter to me. If your company were to be plucked from the face of the earth, I would be distraught and I know the people who work for you would be distraught. I know they love their jobs and that they are well taken care of."

Now I ask people while delivering lectures: "Do you matter? If you were plucked from the face of the earth, would anyone care? Other than your parents, would anyone even show up to your funeral to pay you homage?

I think there is a direct correlation in life between your level of happiness and how much you matter. The more people you matter to, the happier you are going to be in your life.

Therefore, **my definition of success is mattering**. It is knowing that when I leave this earth that there will be people who say "he really mattered. He really made a difference."

—Interview conducted by Seraphina Lin, Cathe Theusch, and David Tauchen, University of Colorado, Boulder

flying high

THE DRUMMER WITH A PLAN

?UESTLOVE
Philadelphia, Pennsylvania
Drummer for The Roots
Accepted to Juilliard, but never attended

?UESTLOVE'S OPEN ROAD MAP

Grows up in Philadelphia; friends were either
"dead or in jail" by 21.

Father pushes him into music at an early age.

Accepted to Juilliard, but could not attend
"due to financial circumstances."

Receives first record deal; "a total fluke."

Releases three more records;
fourth record wins a Grammy.

Label shuts down;
shifted to another label that was "very cold."

Leaves label; relies on "emergency fund"
while searching for new label.

Encourages others to "properly plan out your life."

Proper planning is the answer.

Ahmir Thompson IS THE DRUMMER AND BACKBONE BEHIND THE GRAMMY AWARD–WINNING BAND THE ROOTS. THE GROUP HAS BEEN TOGETHER FOR MORE THAN THIRTEEN YEARS, A RARITY IN THAT FIELD. "MOST GROUPS LAST LESS THAN TEN YEARS—THE BEATLES DID LESS THAN THAT. I THANK GOD WE HAD THE FOCUS TO SEE THAT THERE WAS SOMETHING BETTER THAN WHAT WAS IMMEDIATELY APPARENT. THAT IS WHAT ALLOWED US TO RISE ABOVE THE WATER AND NOT DROWN." AHMIR HAD BEEN UP ALL NIGHT WORKING ON THE ROOTS' NEW ALBUM, BUT HE GREETED US WITH AN ENGAGING WARMTH OF ENERGY. WE SET UP IN HIS RECORD VAULT OF 30,000 RECORDS (HE "ONLY" KNOWS 10,000 BY HEART), WHERE HE SHARED HIS LONG WINDING STORY WITH US.

Everyone who I grew up with on my block was either dead or in jail by the time we turned twenty-one years old. Now none of my friends who I played basketball with growing up are alive—with the exception of those serving time. So I'm grateful for the pressure my father put on me to practice music.

The main crossroads of my life appeared when I was accepted to Juilliard in New York. As much as I wanted to attend Juilliard, I couldn't due to financial circumstances. At that time The Roots were also offered a record deal, which we took because at the end of the day that was the direction I wanted to go anyway.

When I looked at where I was at that time through my father's eyes, I thought I was letting him down even though he was silent. My dad wanted me to do the jazz line with Anita Baker—that was his dream. I didn't even mention a word of The Roots to him until 1992, long after our formation. Even when I got my record deal, he wondered whether it was going to be a real career and thought I should maybe go to college instead. **I was very discouraged**.

Getting our record deal was a total fluke. We were ready to sign with this label, but in 1992 the standard record deal for hip-hop groups was atrocious. De La Soul revealed to me that the budget for their most critically acclaimed album—<u>Three Feet High and Rising</u>—was $25,000. That is the equivalent of walking in late on a Monopoly game when everyone already has properties on the board, someone gives you $25 in pinks and whites, and you end up winning nonetheless. The average recording budget is $250,000 to 500,000, but for $25,000 they created one of the greatest hip-hop records of all time.

We didn't want to end up like that, so thank God for the parents who gave us crazy names. Usually, when you get a contract, there is an opportunity for a lawyer to go through the content and mark something with an initial to fix later. However, because three of our names were misspelled, our lawyer thought we should send it back and request one with the name corrections.

We returned the contract to them, they made the adjustment, and their lawyer told his assistant to FedEx it back to us the next business day—which was Thursday to Friday. The assistant forgot to send the contract. Well, then Friday came and they forgot again. He told us they would send it out Monday. Thank God they didn't think of Saturday FedEx delivery because two hours later my lawyer calls and informs me that Geffen Records is about to start a black music division and the woman who runs the label wanted to see us.

Now, in 1993, the history of Geffen was incredible. They had signed Nirvana. They issued both Guns N' Roses albums. Even their lesser artists, like Aerosmith, were selling 8 million copies worldwide. Between Nirvana, Guns N' Roses, and Aerosmith, they were generating more billions than any other label. It was a "can't lose" situation.

So the lady from Geffen came over, watched us perform, and then took us out to dinner. At dinner I pulled my manager into the bathroom and wanted to know what to do because she looked interested. I thought "let's go for it." So we created the dream laundry list for our record deal. Our list was unprecedented. Nobody in black music had balls enough to, without a record deal, approach a record executive with that list of requests.

The lady from Geffen made a poker face and said, "I'll see what's up." We got a call at 11:00 P.M. on Sunday night from my lawyer. She fell for it, and we were offered the deal.

The record executive of the other label just about had an anxiety attack. We signed with the new Geffen label and I really think we were the last act in hip-hop to be allowed this level of freedom. Geffen explained to us that they didn't know what they were doing (at that time, there was nothing at Geffen but rock and country), but they believed in career artists. They knew that we weren't supposed to trust record executives, but they told us they were not going to fuck us over. All they asked us to do was make a creative record.

With that attitude and freedom, we made <u>Do You Want More?</u> which was highly acclaimed and has sold 400,000 copies, compared to the average underground record, which sells 60,000. It was an album of absolute freedom. Once we did the follow-up record we almost got to gold. Finally, with our fourth album <u>Things Fall Apart</u> (how ironic), we reached jackpot: 900,000 copies sold.

No other hip-hop album without a dance hit had done numbers like that. The primary purpose of hip-hop in the mind of executives is to rock the party. It's to produce a club banger. For us to hit the jackpot on a ballad and win a Grammy against competition like Puffy, R. Kelly, Janet, Dr. Dre and Snoop was unbelievable.

Then I could do the album that I really wanted to do. That was <u>Phrenology</u>. I wanted to show the audience and the critics that we could do much more than your typical three minute verse-and-chorus album. <u>Phrenology</u> was the irony album. We actually made a list of all the things The Roots had never done—a rock song, a techno song, a punk song, a cheesy r & b—and we did it and we won!

We sold 700,000 albums but then the black department at Geffen Records shut down. We got transferred to their sister label, MCA, and then they got shut down. And then we got shifted back to Geffen, but this time we were going under the umbrella of the mighty Interscope label. Interscope at that time was exactly what Geffen had been to rock music when we signed there in 1993. Their least-selling artist was Loretta Lynn and she released one of the most critically acclaimed albums of her career there. Even though they were a department of Geffen, it was a very cold, very numbers-oriented environment. The old Geffen building wasn't even an office building—it was a house and it gave you the feeling of being at home. In contrast, Interscope was very cold.

Through another contract technicality **we got out of the Interscope contract,** and right now, technically we have no label. We are in a bidding war among four labels and the new album will come out in February. It's entitled <u>Game Theory</u>. It's about 80 percent done now, and we are shooting our first video for the single this weekend.

We cannot take the risk of not doing the typical six-month set-up before an album drops, so we have to reach into our own pockets and fund ourselves for now, until we land on terra firma with another label. We have to go to an emergency fund until we settle on a label. Thank God we planned for this. It was Plan D. **Don't ever think that this stuff is ever easy**.

But we didn't always plan this well—when we first started out we didn't know any better. When I got my first record advance, we were playing on the streets of Philadelphia with a shoebox on the sidewalks. If someone put a twenty dollar bill in there, that was Donald Trump city. All we wanted was date money! We wanted to take our girls to the movie theaters and go to McDonald's afterwards. Literally, that is all we wanted to do; to get some attention, take a cute girl out, and go see <u>Children of the Corn</u> Part 3. [Laughs].

When we got our $200,000 advance it was three days before Christmas. We were so stupid back then. It was like a ransom notice. "We want cash and we want fifties and twenties. Have it on the table." We were like Demi Moore in <u>Indecent Proposal</u>. We had never seen this amount of money, we were so stupid, and each took our cut. That was December 23rd and one week after my birthday, January 27th, I think I had $160 left.

I was so stupid, but I'm not afraid to tell that story. I want you to know how stupid I was at twenty-two years old walking down the streets of Philadelphia with $27,000 cash in my backpack. There was no mentor to tell me "You should look up real estate or government bonds so that if you don't make it in 1996, you'll be straight." I wasn't thinking of 1996. It was 1993 and 1996 was forever away and I thought that just as they'd given us $200,000 on the table, they would do it again. Luckily, they gave it to us again, but that is only because we bullet-proofed ourselves by achieving critical acclaim.

I've learned in those thirteen years that it is so much better to properly plan out your life. I know I might go over the top, but I am just that type of person now because I never want to go back to that time in Nice, France, where there were four to a room, suffering, playing to an audience of 13. I don't ever want to do that again. Proper planning is my answer.

I think at the end of the day, I want to be recognized. **There's a difference between acknowledged and recognized**. Acknowledgement comes with fanfare for a king. I will be happy if we are just remembered in the history books.

—Interview conducted by Laura Morris, Mike Wagman, and Coby Shuman, McGill and Concordia University

FROM NSA TO HBO

WANDA SYKES
Portsmouth, Virginia
Stand-Up Comedian
Hampton University

WANDA SYKES'S OPEN ROAD MAP
▼

Has a passion for entertainment, but felt like it was
"too much of a risk."

▼

In college, majors in marketing because
"it seemed safe."

▼

Graduates and goes to work for the NSA;
"not what I wanted to do."

▼

Hears a radio ad for a stand-up open mic night,
decides to give it a try.

▼

Begins to pursue more open mic nights.

▼

After five years, quits the NSA to pursue
stand-up full-time.

There is no greater feeling than doing something you enjoy.

Wanda IS A SUCCESSFUL STAND-UP COMEDIAN, BUT IT WASN'T ALWAYS THAT WAY. SHE BATTLED A STREAK OF BAD SHOWS AND A DOUBTFUL FAMILY EARLY ON, BUT PERSISTED BECAUSE "IT FELT LIKE WHAT I WAS SUP-POSED TO BE DOING." SLOWLY SHE BUILT THE COURAGE TO QUIT HER DAY JOB AT THE NATIONAL SECURITY AGENCY (NSA) AND COMMIT TO COMEDY FULL TIME. TODAY SHE HAS ACHIEVED JUST ABOUT EVERY ACCOLADE POSSIBLE IN THE STAND-UP FIELD—INCLUDING TWO EMMYS—AND HAS BEEN FEATURED ON COMEDY CENTRAL, HBO, FOX, AND IN SEVERAL MAJOR MOTION PICTURES.

I found my passion by being in a job that was a dead-end for me. It was a good job at the National Security Agency (NSA), but I knew it wasn't for me.

I went to college at Hampton University, where I graduated with a degree in marketing. I didn't want to go into marketing, but it looked like the easiest field for me to get a degree in. It seemed safe. I always wanted to do something in entertainment, but I didn't know anyone in the industry. To even contemplate going into that field felt like too much of a risk.

Out of school I lived in the Washington, D.C., area. Being in that area you automatically go to work for the government, so I got a job at the National Security Agency. I was moving up, getting promoted, and receiving awards, but it hit me that this was not what I wanted to do with the rest of my life.

I did not see myself fitting into the typical 9:00 A.M. to 5:00 P.M. culture—getting up, going to work, doing the same thing, coming home, drinking—and doing the same thing over and over again.

Sometimes being in a place where you don't want to be pushes you to roll the dice and go after something you really enjoy.

For me, that was comedy. I had always watched comedy on TV, but I had never been to a comedy club. I heard on the radio that there was a talent show with comedy as a category so **I decided to write some jokes** and go on the show.

Everything opened up from there. I continued to go on stage and I met other comics like Dave Chapelle—we were in clubs at the same time. It was funny because he was so young back then. He was sixteen and if his mom couldn't come to a show he would tell them that I was his aunt so he could hang out. [Laughs].

The more I did it, the more I felt like doing stand-up was why I was put on earth. **It felt right**. Even when it was hard—even when people booed and walked out on me, it didn't make me quit. It felt like what I was supposed to be doing.

For five years I did stand-up at night and worked for the NSA during the day. It wasn't until 1992 that I officially quit the NSA and moved to New Jersey so that I could work out of the New York City clubs. It felt like a risk because at the NSA I was making $40,000 a year, which was a lot back then.

I messed up by inviting my parents to a show way too early in my career. They saw a really bad night. **I bombed silly**. My mother said, "It's okay. You have a good job. You don't have to go through this." When I told them that I was going to leave the NSA and pursue comedy, they thought I had lost my mind.

One time I had a string of bad shows. I went two or three weeks without having a good show. I wasn't pushing myself, and the audience could feel it. At that point I had to dig deeper or give up. The idea of going back to the NSA was the reason I never gave up. Whenever I had doubts about what I was doing—not getting health benefits, etc.—and thought about going back to the NSA, I couldn't do it because I had a taste of what comedy could be like. **It felt like a big, warm, fuzzy blanket that made me so happy.**

There is no greater feeling than making a living doing something you want to be doing. Once you figure that out, you've won! And then everything else you get is just the bonus.

You have to take risks. **Risk is a huge part of it**. I think that's why people are in jobs that they don't want to be in. People are conditioned to get a good job, family, and house—and that's it. We don't think outside the box. We don't dream. That's why you have people shooting up the post office! They don't want to be in the post office! They want to be an artist—they want to do something else.

I didn't ever calculate how much money it would take to make me happy, I just calculated the expenses I had to pay every month and looked at a calendar to see when I had to pay them.

I have been late with the rent, had checks bounce—whatever. I just saw it as needing to pick up a couple more acts.

Say ten years from now you have the house and family you want, but you are miserable and want to run away from it. You're stuck with a big-ass mortgage so you're also stuck with a job you don't like, to pay for the house. You need to think about what's going to make you happy. What is going to make you get up in the morning and <u>want</u> to go to work—and be happy when you come home. I think that families would be happier and healthier if the parents were coming from places where they enjoyed their time. Parents are better when they're not stressed out.

Have a passion and don't look at "status reasons" for doing things. Don't pick your career because it sounds appealing status-wise; like being a doctor or lawyer. Just find the things that make you happy. Have a happy life. Don't think of the money first! Think about what will make you happy first and I guarantee the money will come. **The money will come**.

—Interview conducted by Seraphina Lin, Cathe Theusch, and David Tauchen, University of Colorado, Boulder

MY AMERICAN LIFE

IRA GLASS

Baltimore, Maryland
Host of "This American Life"
on National Public Radio
Attended Northwestern University,
then transferred and graduated from
Brown University

IRA GLASS'S OPEN ROAD MAP

▼

Grows up in "Jewish suburbs of Baltimore";
expected to become a doctor.

▼

In college, works for a hospital
and NPR during summertime.

▼

"It was really clear which one
was more appealing to me."

▼

Continued to work at NPR for free as a tape cutter.

▼

Creates his own segments on the side.

▼

Becomes reporter and host for <u>Morning Edition</u>
and <u>All Things Considered</u>.

▼

Now host and producer of NPR's <u>This American Life</u>.

Surround yourself with ideas.

Ira Glass TRANSFERRED FROM NORTHWESTERN TO BROWN UNIVERSITY BECAUSE HE WAS SICK OF STUDENTS WHO WERE "ONLY INTERESTED IN GRADUATE DEGREES AND MAKING MONEY." SINCE THEN HE'S WORKED IN PUBLIC RADIO FOR MORE THAN TWENTY YEARS—BUT WE LEARNED THAT HE CERTAINLY DIDN'T ALWAYS HAVE IT FIGURED OUT. AT ONE POINT HE WASN'T EVEN VERY GOOD AT WHAT HE DID. HE SHARED WITH US THAT "HARD WORK CAN MAKE A PERSON TALENTED." TODAY IRA IS THE HOST AND PRODUCER OF NPR'S THIS AMERICAN LIFE, A NATIONALLY SYNDICATED RADIO SHOW THAT REACHES 1.6 MILLION LISTENERS EVERY WEEK.

I t's my belief that people tend to be happier when they go for what they want rather than going for what they think they should have.

I grew up in the Jewish suburbs of Baltimore, where if you were smart and capable, you were expected to go to medical school. My parents really wanted me to be a doctor. It didn't even occur to them that there was something else that I could do.

My uncle, who is a doctor, hooked me up with a summer internship at the University of Maryland Hospital. But I didn't have any connection with science or medicine, so that same summer I went looking for a job in radio or advertising. I ended up at National Public Radio in 1978 working for free as a tape cutter. Back then, public radio had only existed as a national network for six years and I had never heard of it. I didn't come from a family that listened to public radio. I never met anyone that did broadcasting or anything creative. It didn't seem conceivable that you could get a job like that.

During that summer I spent half my time at the hospital and half in public radio—so I could directly compare my experiences. At the end of the summer it seemed really clear which one was more appealing to me.

When you try something, some combination of luck and circumstance will step in, and you won't have to choose in the end. That's what happened to me. I feel that you should put yourself in a situation to **try a number of things** and then one of the answers will deliver itself to you.

You don't always have to be talented in something to know it's for you, but you do have to have a couple of skills to propel you. For example, I was always a really good editor. From the beginning, I could put together lovely little six-minute segments from long pieces of work. Even though I was a good editor, **it was not easy for me. I was really bad** in every other part of radio production. I was a terrible writer—it would take me weeks to finish a story. I never moved forward. I was a terrible performer. I had no idea how to be a reporter. So I started at nineteen years old at the network level cutting tapes. At some point I decided to teach myself to be a reporter on the radio. It took me a long time to get there, though. I worked as a temp secretary for years first. I would work very slowly doing a story every two to three months and I gradually got quicker and quicker. I learned that sometimes even with the stuff that you become really good at, you aren't good at it right away.

My parents only told me that it was okay <u>not</u> to go to medical school when I was in my mid-thirties. By then, I already had a national radio show. Throughout my entire twenties, my parents thought every choice I was making was horrible. My dad would try to listen to <u>All Things Considered</u> and just hated it.

It was partly because they were raised with no money at all. They were really poor. Like a lot of people's parents, the drama of their lives was making it to the middle class. It is the whole "American Story." Once they made it to the middle class and achieved financial security, it was difficult for them to imagine a world where that was not the most important thing.

Sadly for them, they had done such a good job making it to the middle class that I was not scared of slipping back into poverty. **I didn't feel worried about making money**.

They were always worried and it took me a really long time to understand their worry. There were many bitter, bitter fights. It's hard when your parents disapprove of you. Obviously, I'm all square with them—it's all worked out—but it took a really long time.

If I could offer you some advice, it would be to **force yourself to work**. Put yourself in a situation where you are forced to turn around product. That is where the skills will come. That is the hardest phase.

Always keep in mind that you just need <u>one</u> break. The rule of thumb in radio is that most people work for nothing for a year or two. You'll work as a temp secretary or something. That's utterly normal. During that time, you have to remember that you don't need to be granted permission to start making work.

A really important part of creative work is coming up with an idea for a story. That's just as much work as actually making stories. It's the same in movies or music. Some people think that if they just sit there, that lightning is going to hit them. That is not how it goes. People who make creative work for a living have to be in a position to make ideas. The rule of thumb is that ideas come from other ideas so you have to immerse yourself in a lot of stuff so that ideas have a chance to come into your head—like books and magazines. Make sure that you are surrounded by ideas.

—Interview conducted by Seraphina Lin, Cathe Theusch, and David Tauchen, University of Colorado, Boulder

DO IT YOURSELF:
HOW TO CREATE YOUR OWN
ROADTRIP EXPERIENCE

NOW IT'S YOUR TURN:
Find the Open Road

HOW DID A COUPLE OF SCRAPPY COLLEGE KIDS BOOK INTERVIEWS WITH SUC-
CESSFUL LEADERS ACROSS THE COUNTRY? THAT'S SOMETHING WE GET ASKED
ALL THE TIME. THIS PART OF THE BOOK ANSWERS THE QUESTION IN THE HOPE
THAT YOU CAN USE WHAT WE LEARNED TO CREATE YOUR OWN VERSION OF OUR
ROADTRIP. IT'S ONE THING TO READ ABOUT OUR ADVENTURES, BUT TO RE-
ALLY UNDERSTAND THE RADICAL IMPACT THIS EXPERIENCE CAN HAVE ON
YOUR LIFE, YOU HAVE TO DO IT YOURSELF.

Y ou may ask yourself, "Why should I go out and interview
people on my own? Why should I explore?" Answer: When you explore, you open your eyes to the many roads that exist. That exposure helps you find paths that connect with your individuality.

If you don't have a broad understanding of what's out there,
how can you really figure out what you want to do with your life?

Not to explore is to limit your choices, and it increases the chances that you'll fall into a path that has nothing to do with what truly lights you up.

One of the best ways to explore the world is to simply ask others how they got to where they are today. Whether it's your barber, one of your mom's college friends, or a CEO that you cold call and take out for coffee, listening to how people have found their paths in life will help you find yours.

Reading the stories of leaders who we profiled is one way to explore, but the world is so much bigger than this book. Millions of people are right now leading amazing lives that you have no idea exist. We can't interview all of them, which is why we created this section: to give you the tools to do it yourself.

While some of these tips will seem obvious, others will be hard to find anywhere else. Take what you like, ignore what you don't. We're just sharing what worked for us.

We know your mission will be different than ours. You probably don't intend to travel around the country in an RV and make a film about it. But you may be in the same situation that we were: utterly clueless about what to do after graduating college. On the other hand, some of you may have an idea where you want to go with your life, but you just don't know where or how to start. Whatever situation you're in, you have a good reason to embark on your own experience.

First, Find Your Red Rubber Ball

Inspired by Nike's Kevin Carroll

For people who don't know what their passion is, the road can be especially dark. That's what meeting with people is all about. The more you listen to others—and expose yourself to all the different paths out there—the easier it is to identify your own passion and figure out how to build your life around it.

One of the best explanations we heard about how to identify your passion came from Nike's Kevin Carroll. Kevin and his brothers were raised by his grandparents and at a young age he found inspiration in sports. Kevin came to symbolize that passion with a red rubber ball—the quintessential playground toy—and sports became his compass. It was behind every decision he made: He joined the Air Force so he could play soccer in Europe; after he got hurt, he studied sports medicine and eventually became a trainer for the Philadelphia 76ers basketball team; and today he's known as "The Katalyst" at Nike. Through it all, Kevin never lost sight of his red rubber ball. Here's what he told us:

"Where do **dreams** start?
They start when you're free to romp and run
around. That's when you begin to imagine
that you're **something bigger** than you are.
The red rubber ball represents play to me. It represents
what makes me excited about the day.
So **ask yourself**, 'What is my red rubber ball?'
What is the one thing that, if it was taken away,
would make you paralyzed or stuck?
What is that thing that **brings you joy?**"

Consider the people we interviewed: Mike Lazzo's red rubber ball is television. Beth McCarthy Miller's rubber ball is entertainment. Manny the Lobsterman's ball is being out on the ocean. Leigh Steinberg's is helping athletes.

Once you identify your passion, the road can still seem daunting. How do you turn that passion into your life's work? How do you tap into the television business? How can you make a living as a writer? How do you avoid spending your days trapped behind a desk?

That's why you need to hit the road. Asking other people how they found their path in life will help you find yours.

Is your red rubber ball dancing? Call up the choreographer of your favorite music video. Is your ball food? Call up a producer at the Food Network. Is it animals? Interview someone—anyone—at Sea World! One conversation over coffee might be just the spark you need to find the open road.

So, Whom Should You Meet?

Answer: **Anyone you want.**

    Interested in starting your own business? Think of success-ful people you admire, like we did with Redhook Ale Brewery founder Paul Shipman. Or start with the owner of a business in your hometown. Love to take pictures and travel? Talk to some-one from <u>National Geographic</u>. Obsessed with basketball? Call someone who works for the National Basketball Association. You can talk to anyone: your best friend's dad, your dentist's next-door neighbor, the woman sitting next to you in the coffee shop, or the person who designs Madonna's clothes.

Keep your **ear to** the ground.
Interesting people to interview are all around you.
They're in line at the grocery store,
profiled in a magazine, and **listed**
in the **credits** of a movie.

We suggest you start with the simple goal of meeting ten people. Begin with your hobbies. Do you love photography, writing, or surfing the Web? Pick three people who are in some way related to it, like a photographer, a newspaper reporter, or the founder of your favorite Web site. Don't worry if you're not fired up to follow their exact footsteps. Just meet with them and hear their stories.

Second, pick three people who are in an area that you <u>think</u> you might be interested in: advertising, marketing, the Internet, not-for-profit, social work, fashion design, engineering, whatever. These folks will give you the real scoop on what it's like to work, day to day, in a specific field and what you need to break in. You might learn it's not what you envisioned.

Third, pick three wild cards. These are people you never imagined that you'd meet but consider impressive and interesting: a movie producer, an Olympic speed skater, a scientist, a construction worker, the chief executive of a multibillion-dollar company, an orchestra conductor. Again, don't worry about whether you can picture yourself in their shoes. Just trust that the insights they'll share about their own experiences can translate to your life.

That leaves one more interview to plan. Let someone else pick this person for you. This should be a truly serendipitous meeting. For us it was Manny the Lobsterman, whom we stumbled upon while we roadtripped across Maine. He turned out to be one of the most fascinating, inspirational, down-to-earth people on our trip.

Why Me?

"Why would anyone want to meet with me?"

That's what we thought at first. After all, we were just two surfers from Laguna Beach with no idea what to do with our lives.

But remember this: Older people were once young and frantic about the future, too. Most got help from others along the way. So when someone like you calls and asks for their time, they are often excited to share their stories with a young person determined to pave his or her own road.

Most people **enjoy**
telling their stories
and rarely have someone
who wants to listen.

How to Find People

Start with people you know. Your Uncle Bob may be a total bore and has a job you hate, but don't write him off. The guy may know other people who have walked down roads that may light you up.

We asked the chancellor of our college if he knew of anyone who was interesting to interview. He referred us to Tommy Lasorda, the former general manager of the Los Angeles Dodgers, and Howard White, who manages the Michael Jordan brand at Nike. After about a million calls, we were able to meet both of them. Our point is this:

Ask everyone you know if they know anyone with whom you can meet to aid your exploration.

Being referred by someone is a lot easier than making a cold call. Most people will agree to meet you if, for example, their college buddy Bob told you about them. Here's a quick list of sources to get you started:

Parents and siblings	**Past employers**
Relatives	**Your doctors**
Friends and friends' parents	**Parents' neighbors and friends**
High school teachers	**College professors**
College alumni office	**Sorority or fraternity alumni**

Remember Madonna's stylist Arianne Phillips? She got the name of one of New York's top fashion photographers from her mother's friend.

As for finding people with whom you have absolutely no connection (like almost everyone we met), the key is to pay attention. People with amazing roads that you may want to call your own are all around you. Every cool organization has a founder, leader, and hip employees. Every CD cover has lists of people who made it happen. Every movie you see has hundreds of professionals listed in the credits. Every product has an inventor and a company behind it. Do you like smoothies? Call someone from Jamba Juice. Obsessed with PlayStation? Dial up Sony in San Francisco and ask to speak with one of the game's designers. Love to snowboard? Call Jake Burton and ask what it took to start and successfully grow Burton Snowboards and define a culture.

No one is out of reach
until they tell you so.

Be Resourceful

Magazines and the Internet are your best and easiest bets here. We spent hours camped out at magazine stands just searching for interesting people we could cold call.

HOW TO FIND STRANGERS

Flip through magazines.

↓

Surf the Internet.

↓

Read newspapers.

↓

Watch a variety of television shows.

↓

Check credits of movies, CDs, or books.

We found some really cool people in <u>Rolling Stone</u>, <u>GQ</u>, and <u>Entertainment Weekly</u>. Magazines like <u>Outside</u> will profile people who have pivotal roles in the outdoor recreation industry. You may not be used to reading business publications, but they're not as boring as you think. After all, companies are filled with people who do fascinating things. Profiling them are what publications like <u>The Wall Street Journal</u>, <u>Fast Company</u>, <u>Forbes</u>, <u>Fortune</u>, and <u>BusinessWeek</u> are all about.

Don't forget your local newspapers. The Internet is also a rich source. Check out online news sites like Salon.com, CNET, and CNN.com.

> On most of
> your favorite Web sites,
> if you click on "**About Us**,"
> you'll find a handful of people
> who work at the site.

As you flip through magazines and troll the Web, write down the names of people who spark your interest.

How to Reach Strangers

If your uncle refers you to someone, he'll probably give you the person's phone number. Going after people you don't know, like the director of a television show, is trickier but can be done. All it takes is perseverance and the wherewithal to dial directory assistance.

When we stumbled across an article about Beth McCarthy

Miller in <u>Entertainment Weekly</u>, we called 411 and asked the operator for the main number of <u>Saturday Night Live</u>'s offices in New York City. We were connected to NBC and, flash-forward after three months of persistence, we were sitting in the writers' conference room at the studio and hanging out with Beth.

Company Web sites are also a good source of contacts. You can find the company's headquarters and its main number. Just call and ask for the office of the person you want to meet.

HOW TO MANEUVER A MAGAZINE STAND

Go by your interests. Does surfing light you up? Check out <u>Surfer</u> magazine. Like clothes? Read <u>Vogue</u>. Food? Flip through all the food publications. Sure, these mags are usually filled with surfing adventures, fashion layouts, or cooking recipes, but they often profile very colorful people. You'll find roads you never knew existed. In <u>Fast Company</u> magazine we found an article about Arianne Phillips, a stylist for Madonna. The article included her email address, which is very rare, so we emailed and asked if we could grab coffee with her. She agreed.

So, whom should you meet?

Getting the Meeting

Once you've found a cool cat that you want to sit down with and you have all the contact info, take the next big step. Call 'em up! This is no doubt the most nervewracking part. Whether you cold call a CEO or start up a conversation with a guy in a coffee shop, it takes guts. (Check out "Raw Nerve" in the Appendix.) Our advice here is simple:

The worst thing that can happen is that people say no.

And they will. But who really cares? If they aren't hip enough to take even fifteen minutes to meet with someone ambitious enough to seek them out, they aren't worth your time. It turns out that this is a self-selecting process. The people who agree to meet you are usually the best interviews because they understand that all you're trying to do is figure out your future.

Do not call the company's human resources or public relations department. PR and HR are the Bermuda Triangle of cold calls, and you're more likely to get stopped in your tracks. Ask directly for the person you want. That said, if you must chat with the PR reps, be extremely polite.

The Cold Call . . . Hello?

Think of it as a <u>warm</u> call. It's less daunting and, after all, your goal is to <u>warm</u> people to your story. Once you dial the number, the roller coaster begins. You have no idea who will answer the phone. It could be someone's personal secretary, a company operator, voice mail, or the very person you are trying to reach. Always assume the latter, and be prepared.

In reality, you'll probably get an administrative assistant. We cannot stress this enough:

Administrative assistants hold the keys to the kingdom. Treat them like gold!

Don't blow them off or be bitchy. They're smart and influential or they wouldn't be working for successful people. The few minutes you spend talking to assistants can be your most valuable. After all, they'll be the ones selling your request to the person you want to meet. If you don't make friends with the assistant—or at least get them on your side—it will be tough to move forward. The assistants have the power. Be sure you respect them.

The Pitch

Take a deep breath and remember this: You're not selling anything and you're not asking people to spend money or give you a job. You're simply in search of advice about how to build your future, and that's a damn good mission.

That said, relax. When you get someone on the phone, be yourself. Sometimes we threw in an ice-breaking comment—maybe we asked the assistant how he or she was or cracked a joke. (Note: Jokes early in the morning do not work. Before 10:00 A.M. it's best just to get to the point.)

Your pitch explains who you are and why you're calling. If someone referred you, throw the name in up front: "Bob Smith gave me Mr. Big's number and suggested I call."

If this is a true cold call, you can write out a thirty-second speech that gets your message across. It's a good idea, but don't just read it. Use it as a starting point. Here's what we usually said:

"Hi. My name's Mike Marriner and I'm a student at Pepperdine University. I'm a biology major and I like science but do not want to spend my whole life working with test tubes. I'm exploring what to do with my life, and I saw an article about Beth McCarthy Miller that said she once considered a career in science. I was wondering if she could spare a few minutes of her time just to talk to me about her path and how she ended up becoming the director of <u>Saturday Night Live</u>."

We admit that in most cases we also talked about our project, Roadtrip Nation, and explained that we were driving around the country meeting with dozens of successful people for a possible documentary. It helped to be associated with a project, and in some cases that is probably what got us in the door. But for the most part, people told us they were simply impressed with our enthusiasm and initiative. And, again, many were empathetic to our dilemma.

As for your pitch, two suggestions: First, use our Roadtrip Network to help you get an interview. The network is a community that we set up in which students go out, interview leaders, and then record online what they took away from the experience. We give you permission to use our names! (To learn more about the Roadtrip Network, go to www.roadtrip nation.com.) Your pitch can go something like this:

> "Hi. My name is Amy Bush and I'm a member of the Roadtrip Network. It's a movement of students who interview leaders to learn how their roads from college might help us define our own paths. We then share the experience with an entire generation of young people at roadtripnation.com. I would love to include Oprah in the project. Do you think she could spare any time to meet with me at her convenience?"

The second way to pitch yourself can simply be about your own personal mission:

"Hi. My name is Coralie Simmons and I'm a senior at Indiana University, majoring in English. I'm exploring my options, but I have a lot of unanswered questions and was hoping to speak to Ms. Davis about her own path. I read about her in an article in <u>National Geographic</u> and was fascinated by her work. I know she's terribly busy, but I was hoping she could spare twenty minutes to see me. I'll buy the coffee."

Final pointers: Ask for twenty minutes at least three weeks away. Who can't spare that? Inevitably you'll end up staying for at least half an hour. Finally, with every request:

Emphasize that you are not asking for a job and that you just want to learn about the person's road.

That takes the pressure off. If people know that you don't expect a job and are just looking for input, they'll feel more comfortable meeting with you.

The Response

After the pitch, it's like going fishing. If you get a nibble, give a little tug. If you don't get much of a response, change your bait and try describing what you want from a different angle. For example, narrow your pitch by saying that you really want to break into the specific industry. Ask if they can suggest anyone else at the company you can call, other than the human resources department.

A lot of times we'd be interested in a specific company, like Patagonia, and we'd ask the company's main operator, "Who's the coolest person in your company?" Then we'd follow up with the pitch. It caught them off guard and sometimes got a little chuckle. Once they tell you who the coolest person is, be sure to get his or her name so when you get transferred you can say, "Rod Smith told me you were the coolest person in the company to talk to." So what if Rod Smith is the operator!

WHAT TO SAY TO A STRANGER

Introduce yourself.
↓
Say who referred you or how you got his or her name.
↓
Explain your dilemma/situation.
↓
State your request.
↓
Be clear that you're not asking for a job.

We were interested in talking to an architect but had no idea who the stars were. So we called up the industry association and asked for names of the coolest architects in Chicago. When we called these people, we said we were referred by someone from the association.

COLD CALL POINTERS

Never call on a Monday.

↓

Avoid leaving a voice mail until necessary.

↓

Leave a succinct message.

↓

Be patient. They may not call back right away.

↓

Know when to give up!

↓

Avoid the PR and human resources departments.

↓

Follow up ASAP.

Really listen to what people say and respond accordingly.

Your goal is to quickly turn this phone call into a conversation rather than a sales pitch. Tell them about yourself and how you got the idea to call.

Don't hang out too long on the phone. Initiate the close and ask when might be a good time to follow up. Be flexible with your schedule, have some suggested times ready, and know when you absolutely can't meet. It may be tough to reschedule if you have to cancel.

Persistence vs. Annoyance

There is a fine line between persistence and annoyance. Don't cross it. When you call, try to get someone live on the phone because most people won't respond to a voice mail from someone they don't know, unless someone they do know referred you. To get the person live, we sometimes called five times a day but didn't leave a message. If you keep getting voice mail, it's fine to leave a succinct message. Give people a day to call you back before you try again. How many times should you try before you give up? It's up to you, but we sometimes left two messages a week for several months before we quit. In the big scheme of things, it only takes about two minutes a week to keep on it (or slightly longer if you leave long, verbose messages like Mike).

Never call on a Monday. Trust us. People often don't want to be at work on Mondays, let alone take calls from some kid who is not critical to their work. Even if you have the most fired-up, energetic pitch, you'll still have a tough time—just because it's Monday. Our favorite times to call are Wednesday, Thursday, and Friday afternoons. People are winding up the week and are more laid back.

You'll likely be asked to send more information about yourself. Have a one-page letter ready to fax or email (see sample, page 216). The sooner you send it the better. If you say you'll fax it within the hour, *fax it in twenty minutes!* We can't stress enough how important it is to do what you say if you want people to take you seriously. Finally, call to make sure that what you sent arrived. Besides, it's a good excuse to get your request in front of them again.

When we faxed a letter to Michael Dell, Nathan stuck his face on a copier machine and used the image as our cover sheet. He used whiteout to write our contact information. Crazy, but at least we caught their attention.

Faxing Can Be Fun!

First, a warning: Take great care with everything you send to other people. It's indicative of who you are. Misspelled words, messy writing, wrong titles—game over!

Think about how many faxes and emails people get each day. We tried to be creative and make our faxes stand out so they wouldn't get lost in the mass of standard stuff.

We are also huge fans of exclamation points. It conveyed our excitement and passion. But be careful—they can backfire if overused. Some people can misinterpret how serious you are. Point: Be creative, but don't go overboard. (Check out "Stake Out" in the Appendix.)

There's **a fine line** between creativity and insanity.

You want your communication to stand out, but don't overdo it. Express yourself, sure, but use common sense and consider your audience. We probably would not have faxed Nate's face to Supreme Court Associate Justice Sandra Day O'Connor.

When we emailed Alan Webber, the cofounder of Fast Company magazine, Nathan titled the email "Don't read this!!!" Whether or not that was what triggered him to read our note, we'll never know, but Alan sat down to talk with us a month or so later.

Email Strategy

Instead of calling, you may opt to send an email. When you email people who have no clue who you are, the biggest challenge is getting them to open your note. So get creative with your subject heading. You can describe your mission, like "Lunch with cool people," or something a bit more outrageous.

Of course, today people are scared to open emails from strangers for fear of computer viruses. Just ask yourself this about your subject line: Would you open it? Also, keep your email short. You have a second to catch your readers' attentions—and if it even looks long, they'll abandon ship. Get to the point and include all the critical information on one screen view. Put the noncritical stuff in a postscript.

What to Write

The content of any fax, email, or letter is essentially the same. You want to introduce yourself and explain why you are contacting people in a way that makes them say, "Wow!" This can be done in several ways, but it should reflect your personal style. Following are some suggestions.

Make it a story— get personal!

People are more likely to read stories than proposals. Make your one-pager personal. Talk about your situation, what obstacles you face, and how a meeting with that person could help you get over those hurdles.

OUTLINE OF A LETTER

··

INTRODUCTION: HOW YOU FOUND THE PERSON

Dear————

   • I recently read an article about you in <u>Time</u> magazine and was fascinated by your story.
   • My uncle, Matthew Berk, suggested that I contact you.
   • I've been a fan of yours for years.
   • I'm a huge fan of Nike gear.

SECOND PARAGRAPH: YOUR STORY

   • I'm a junior at Loyola University, currently studying marketing, but I'm unsure just what path to pursue after college. I need to expose myself to all the possibilities and the only way to do that is to get out and talk to people like yourself.
   • I was planning on going to law school but, despite pressure from my parents, I decided it's not for me. When I read that you had switched from a legal career to business, I knew I had to hear your story of discovery!
   • I'm a biology major but have no desire to get stuck working in a lab for my whole life, and I definitely don't want to go to medical school. I'm exploring different ways to use biology or apply my writing skills.
   • I've worked on my school newspaper for four years and love covering and discovering local bands. I desperately want to be a music reporter, but I have no idea how to break into the field.
   • I'm part of a national movement called Roadtrip Nation,

where young people who are intent on leading fulfilling lives meet with people like yourself and listen to how they got from high school or college to where they are now.

THIRD PARAGRAPH: WHAT YOU WANT (AND DON'T WANT)

I'm not looking for a job at this point, but I am...

• ...trying to sit down with accomplished people like yourself and learn from their experiences. I'd be grateful if you could spare a few minutes of your time one day to share your story with me.

• ...interested in how you figured out your own road since college. I'd love to hear your story.

• ...looking for some advice about how to break into the marketing industry.

CLOSING: SPECIFIC MEETING REQUEST

• If you can spare twenty minutes one afternoon, I'd love to stop by your office and hear how you got to where you are. I'll buy the coffee! I'll follow up with a phone call in a few days, or feel free to call me at 310-555-1212.

Scheduling the Interview

The timing of the interview is also important. At the beginning of the week, people tend to be more hectic and their minds are consumed with what they have to accomplish in the days ahead. If you can snag someone for a late afternoon lunch near the end of

getting the meeting

the week, say about 1:30 P.M. on a Thursday, great. A 12:00 P.M. lunch on Tuesday will usually mean a rushed meal. Another option is the half-hour, late-afternoon coffee. Offer to bring coffee to their office or to meet them nearby. People are usually ready to take a break at about three or four o'clock.

If all else fails, the I-can-drop-by-your-office-for-twenty-minutes-whenever-you-have-time pitch is a difficult request to turn down.

If your request for a meeting is declined, it's no biggie. Chalk it up as a successful failure. Hey, at least you called! If they're rude, and some people will be, thank them for their time in a polite voice and move on. Their loss.

OUR FAVORITE MEETING OPTIONS

- Wednesdays, Thursdays, or Fridays
- Lunchtime
- Late-afternoon coffee
- The twenty-minute meeting at their office

When you do book an interview, it's a huge rush. On top of that, you'll feel intense anticipation for a fresh experience that could provide critical guidance on how to forge your own road in life.

Preparing for the Interview

You booked the interview. Right on.

Now you've got to get ready for it. Don't worry. It's not as much work as studying for a test or writing your thesis. But you don't want to look like a complete idiot when you walk into someone's office.

A great source of information is the person's administrative assistant— yet another reason to treat them like gold.

Here's a good question to ask an assistant: "Why do you think your boss has been so successful?" Then, just listen. You may learn how long the leaders have been doing what they do best, their reputation around the workplace, their personality, and about their life outside work. These folks can also send you a resume or bio.

If you don't already know what the company does, find out. To be honest, we did not do as much company research before each meeting as we could have. But it definitely helps to have some idea of how a company is doing. If it just declared bankruptcy, wouldn't you like to know?

OTHER GOOD SOURCES OF
COMPANY AND INDIVIDUAL INFORMATION

Google, Yahoo!—These search engines will dig up online articles about the company, as well as the person you are meeting.

Industry trade magazines—Every industry has its own magazines. From aerospace to zoos, if it's a business, it has a publication. They're not available on newsstands, so check at a library.

Business magazines—Business magazines cover just about any interest you can think of. Check out The Wall Street Journal, BusinessWeek, Forbes, Fortune, Barron's, Fast Company.

Books—Before we interviewed Paul Shipman, the CEO and founder of Redhook Ale Brewery, we skimmed through Redhook: Beer Pioneer, a book about his past. Most people you meet with will not have books written about them, but it's worth a quick search online or at your local bookstore.

Go to the company's Web site and poke around.

Once on a company Web site, we went straight to the "press" section. It's a great place to get company-provided information. Senior executives will often have their resumes or work histories posted online. If the company's stock is publicly traded, the "investor relations" section of the site will have a copy of the annual report, which tells you about the company. Also check out press releases to get an idea of recent news. Some sites have links to related articles and profiles about top executives.

It's good to do some general research about the company, but try to focus your research on the individual. This not only shows respect for the people you meet but it steers your conversation in the direction of their personal stories and how they got where they are today.

Of course, if all you're interested in is a company's financials, you don't need a meeting. Use the interview to dig up experiences that you can't find anywhere else.

In the Meeting

"What the Hell Do I Talk About?"
Do not go into the meeting with a laundry list of predetermined
questions like we did before we slid into our interview groove. In
the early days, we stuck to a one-page list of forty questions. Big
mistake! It probably felt more like an interrogation than a conversation for the poor people we initially interviewed. Solution?
Have five open-ended questions as your guideposts, but be flexible (see page 223 for examples.)

Let your curiosity guide you.

The conversation will take on a life of its own, so be flexible
as you ride its many twists and turns. There are no right questions or right answers. That's 90 percent of the fun! You never
know what topic or wild anecdote you'll stumble across. Ride the
tangents or you'll miss a ton of great stuff.

The real magic of the interviews comes from the tangents themselves.

That said, remember this: You're the one in control of the dialogue. If you don't want to waste time talking about, say, someone's kids or their stamp collection, move on. Ask another question. Following are some suggested questions you may want to pick from.

Suggested Questions

We typically walked into each interview with two specific questions in mind. From there the conversation took off, and we rode the tangents.

1. Where were you when you were our age, and how did you get from there to where you are today?

2. If you had one piece of advice to young people getting ready to jump into the real world, what would it be?

Burson-Marsteller's chief executive, Chris Komisarjevsky, told us that when he left college it was really scary because of the Vietnam War. Rather than skip that topic, we dove in and asked him how he got through those tough years. He told us that the intense experience gave him amazing leadership training and taught him how to perform under pressure. It was stuff we'd never have known unless we'd asked.

Of course, you have to be careful when asking sensitive questions and know when to back off. If Chris had shrugged off our questions about Vietnam or looked uncomfortable, we would have switched topics.

The first question gets them talking about their past and how their journey began. Whatever they say will spark more questions from you.

SAMPLE QUESTIONS

Each question you ask opens a door to insights that will help you define your own road. We have two types of sample questions: *inspirational* and *informational*.

Use <u>inspirational</u> interview questions if you're still searching for your road—which you probably are. The second batch, <u>informational</u> questions, is more focused. If you have some sense of what you want to do with your life and the person you're interviewing is in that industry, these questions will help you to explore the ins and outs of that path a little better. They'll help you determine if that road is right for you.

In our interviews, we used a mix of both types of questions. Sometimes we went broad and sometimes we got into specifics. It depends on the interview's flow and what you want to get out of the experience.

> <u>Inspirational questions</u> help you find your own passion.
>
> <u>Informational questions</u> help you build a life around your passion.

INSPIRATIONAL QUESTIONS

What were you doing at my age?
Michael Dell dropped out of the University of Texas to start Dell Computer, a move that was seen as a failure at that point in his life. It seems to be working fine now.

Were you ever lost?
After college Howard Schultz, chairman of Starbucks, worked for Xerox but knew he was destined to start his own business— he just didn't know what it would be. It wasn't until he traveled

to Italy and stumbled across the "romance of the Italian espresso bar" that he knew what he wanted to build.

Were there ever pressures from society telling you to be something or do something else? If so, how did you shed the noise?

Paul Shipman, founder and CEO of Redhook Ale Brewery, came from a family of lawyers. When asked this question he said, "When it came to going to law school . . . it was like, you didn't even ask." Instead he chose his own path.

When you were growing up did you have any interests that you have built into your work?

When Beth McCarthy Miller, the director of Saturday Night Live, was young, she directed skits for school assemblies. It's not so different from what she does today, except she has a slightly larger live audience.

When did the lightbulb go on? When did you realize this is what you wanted to do?

Ben Younger, writer and director for the movie Boiler Room, worked as a low-level production assistant on movies when, he says, he first fell in love with the set. A few years later he directed his own film.

What obstacles have you overcome to get to where you are today?

U.S. Supreme Court Associate Justice Sandra Day O'Connor was the first woman ever appointed to the Supreme Court. But many years earlier, when she graduated Stanford Law School, female lawyers were unheard of. Her first job? Working for free next to the secretary at a law firm.

What has been the key to achieving the level of excellence that you've reached in your life?

Manny the Lobsterman in Maine, attributes his happiness to finding a lifestyle that integrates his true passion, the sea, into each day.

How do you balance your personal and professional life?

Rick Allen, CEO of National Geographic Ventures, told us, "Always bet on the family."

As you look back on your first ten years after college, what would you do differently?

Very few people have regrets about their roads. Many were lost, but they look back on that time in their lives as almost an inevitable part of their success. The crucial part was their perspective. They always followed what fired them up.

INFORMATIONAL QUESTIONS

Describe a typical day in the life of your job.

Chuck Armstrong, the president of the Seattle Mariners, said he spends his days working out of his offices at Safeco Field, overseeing team personnel and, of course, watching games from his skybox (which is where we interviewed him).

What skills must someone absolutely have to succeed in your field?

Tom First, the cofounder of Nantucket Nectars, believes that people need a good dose of persistence to start a company.

How did you acquire the necessary skills and knowledge?

When Laurie Coots was determined to get a job at advertising agency Chiat/Day, she took a job as a secretary for the Apple account. She knew nothing about technology, so she read books and learned on the job.

If someone wants to be you, do you suggest that they follow your footsteps?

Seattle Mariners President Chuck Armstrong got to where he is by such a crazy road that he suggests people must pave their own path. "You get to these things by very circuitous routes," he told us.

How can I tap into your field?

Jennifer Rudolph Walsh, a literary agent at the William Morris Agency, suggests starting at the bottom. There are always open jobs in the mailroom, and some of the top people in her field started there.

Is there anyone else that you suggest I talk to?

This is a great question to end with. It's very important for you to get names of two or three other people. A referral almost guarantees you a meeting—and no cold calling!

Jump Start a Stalled Conversation

Most interviews don't start off on a hyper-inspirational level.

Think about it. The people you meet with are very busy. Your job is to make the experience more than just another item on their to-do list, to make it a refreshing break in their day when they can sit down, loosen up, and share the story of how they got to where they are today.

The good news is that just asking questions and being an active listener should drive the conversation. Make sure you look interested and not bored. Also, be real. Be personal. Be humorous if it comes naturally to you. Don't whine, but be honest about your anxieties and the struggles you face in defining your own road. This approach should elicit a similar reaction in them and, hopefully, take the conversation to a personal, more stimulating level.

Sometimes it won't work. Let's say you've set this personal tone up front and the interview is still not reaching that deeper level. The leader is still in corporate mode. How do you get them talking about themselves, not just the job or the industry? Ask more specific, open-ended questions that elicit personal stories regarding how they figured out their futures. For example:

When you were a kid, what did you want to do with your life?

Share an experience when people around you pressured you to be someone or do something.

Give me an example of how you got over those barriers.

Tell me about your first job after college.

When you get them in storytelling mode, the conversation tends to pick up. Stories have more color, are fun to recall, and inevitably make the discussion more personal than professional.

Here's another tip: Don't race through your own list of questions.

Listen carefully to what the leaders answer and ask new questions based on what they tell you.

When we first interviewed Howard Schultz, the chairman of Starbucks, he had just wrapped up a television interview on CNBC during which he talked about Starbucks' financial projections. For the first ten minutes of our conversation, he told us more about the company than his own personal road. He was still in TV mode. We launched into a series of questions that put him back in his youth, and the interview switched gears. Howard's eyes lit up as he reminisced about growing up in Brooklyn. He walked us down the road of his life, with all the speed bumps and triumphs that he had encountered.

This will elicit more information and lead to even more questions. For example, if a leader says that his father really wanted him to go to law school, don't just nod—ask why. Ask what his father did for a living. Ask what influenced his father's road. Ask how they resolved their differences. Ask what his father thinks of him today. You get the idea. Let every answer spark a fresh query.

Interview Etiquette

You don't have to be boring to be polite. We always tried to convey our energy, enthusiasm, and craziness, but we were also courteous and stayed within appropriate boundaries.

Get directions—twice. You absolutely have to show up on time. So get written directions from at least two people. Bring a cell phone in case you get lost. If you're meeting someone at their place, try to arrive fifteen minutes early. If you're interviewing someone at a company, hanging out in the lobby for a few minutes tells you a lot about the company's vibe. We always got there early and poked around.

Imagine trying to find parking for a forty-foot RV in downtown Manhattan, or pulling up to the Supreme Court building during the D.C. anthrax scare in our suspicious-looking bright-green machine with a big trailer on the back. Our advice? Be prepared for anything and aim to get there an hour early!

Explain yourself again. The person you're meeting with is very busy and may not even recall why you are there. Assume she knows nothing. Do your interviewee a favor and launch into your pitch. Try to generate the same excitement you did when you first called the company. Create a sense that this should be a fun conversation for both of you.

> "Thanks so much for taking the time to see me today. I've been so excited to have a chance to talk to you. Let me tell you again why I'm here. I'm graduating in June with a biology degree, but I have no desire to go into a scientific field so I'm trying to figure out all the different paths that my life can take. I believe the best way to do this is to talk with people like yourself and learn from their own life stories. I was

so impressed with the article that I read about you in
<u>W</u> magazine that I wanted to hear your own tale."

It's good to be a bit specific and express interest in some-one's industry. If you're interviewing the editor of <u>Surfer</u> maga-zine, tell him that you surf (assuming that you do, of course). This is also a good time to clarify that you are <u>not</u> there for a job, but to listen.

Be yourself. Act in a way that is most comfortable to you. If you're not a comedian, don't tell a joke. But hey, if it feels right to whip out a few icebreakers, go for it.

Listen. Try to get a sense of how people are responding to you. If they are super-professional, mimic their style to make them more comfortable. If they are incredibly laid back, take more lib-erties with your questions.

Be sensitive to their time constraints. Some days people will have more time to spend with you than others. If they're on a tight schedule, their answers will proba-bly be curt and to the point. Some people will have time to ramble. It's up to you to figure this out and to let them get back to their work if they need to. Even a quick, fifteen-minute meeting can reveal valuable infor-mation, and they'll appreciate that you respected their time.

JACKASS

When we were in the lobby waiting to interview the president of Nordstrom, some guy asked us what the cameras were for. Mike, who is notorious for his in-appropriate jokes, threw out that we were from the MTV show <u>Jackass</u>. The guy got this horrified look on his face, like we were there to do some real damage to his company. It turned out that the man was actually Blake Nordstrom, the CEO of the company and brother of Pete Nordstrom, who we were there to see. Our ad-vice? Be yourself, but shed the stupid jokes.

Be confident, not cocky. This is not a job interview, so the pressure is off. You have only two goals. First, listen to others because they know a lot more than you about their paths. Respect their experience and accept your lack of it. Second, you want them to leave the interview thinking, "Wow, it was a refreshing break in my day talking to that cool person." You don't want them to leave thinking that they wasted their time with a stuck-up know-it-all.

Be enthusiastic, not annoying. People respect others who show initiative and energy. You're already halfway there because the mere fact that you showed up will impress someone. Think of how many other people are sitting home watching TV when they could be chatting with the director of a television show.

Be real. Don't be afraid to talk about fun stuff, like how you got lost on the way there or the art hanging on the office walls.

Be prepared to talk about yourself. Most people will ask you a bit about yourself. Have a brief explanation ready, one that communicates your background and interests. Being personal, open, and real will set the table for a very genuine conversation. Every action elicits an equal and opposite reaction. It's like physics, conversation style.

On the flip side, we often spent too much time talking about ourselves. You want people to know a bit about you, but remember, your main purpose is to find out about them! Don't do all the talking. If you hear yourself talking too much, shut up.

Dress to show respect but still be you. No, you don't have to dress like you're going in to interview for an accounting job. Keep the three-piece suit in the closet where it belongs. We

were ultra slackers but, to be honest, we got away with it because we were living in an RV for three months. That said, be
yourself and wear something clean, neat, and somewhat put together. When in doubt, it's always better to overdress than un-
derdress.

Can I take notes? Sure, as long as it's not distracting.
You're not going to be tested on this information, but if you feel
the need to jot down a few awesome pieces of advice that you
hear, do it. If you can, it's always great to use a voice or video
camera recorder and forget about the notes so you can just con-
centrate on what's being said. Just ask them first if it's okay.

Pay for it. If you go for coffee or lunch, offer to treat. It
could be the best $3, or $30, you'll ever spend.

Closing

In those few minutes, you've received insight that it took someone years to accumulate. Dispense a healthy dose of thanks. No need to kiss their butt. Just convey your sincere appreciation for their time and advice. A few thoughts:

End the meeting on a note that encourages a future relationship. A simple "I would love to stay in touch via email and keep you posted on my progress" is fine. Or "Do you mind if I call you if I have any more questions?" We are huge believers in the power that a mentor can have on your life. Don't destroy a potentially life-changing relationship by not sowing the seeds for future contact.

If the meeting is really successful, the person you interviewed will actually thank you. After our interview with Chuck Wright, the chief marketing officer at State Farm Insurance, he thanked us because he had such a good time thinking through all the concepts he shared. Most people never get a chance to do this in a typical workday. If they thank you, you know you've done a good job.

Jot it down. Keep a small notebook and as soon as you leave the meeting write down what you discussed, what inspired you, and any thoughts you have. This will help you remember the meeting in the future, especially if you ever want to call the person again.

Yeah, you must send a thank you note. Don't send an email. Send a real letter. Write it and pop it in the mail right away. You can hand write it if you want or, if you got a sense that the person would probably appreciate a more professionally typed letter, do that. Keep it brief, refer to a few points you discussed (look at the notes you wrote after the meeting), be sincere, and share how hearing their story has helped you to shape your own.

Try to turn the interview into a mentoring relationship. In all of our interviews, we heard over and over again how mentors were the foundation for so many people's success. Mentors teach you the rules of the game, connect you with people vital to your road, and act as a crucial sounding board when you must make pivotal decisions. One interview is great, but the potential to turn that one meeting into a lifelong mentoring relationship can change your life forever.

Appendix:

Feedback
from the Road

Simon Maude

UK Team

Summer 2005 Roadtrip Reflection

I left school with no idea what I wanted to be. I liked some of the subjects I had studied, but I had no idea what I wanted to do with them. So I floundered around for four years, trying out jobs and careers, in an attempt to find my path in life. I even went to the University of Wellington in New Zealand to study history and anthropology on a one-year try-out basis. But nothing jumped out as my calling in life, and I ended up working in the music industry back in London. I was doing well for myself, and my success made me think that I was happy. I wasn't sure whether I'd be happy there in ten-years' time, but people being impressed with my work and the rock-and-roll lifestyle kept a smile on my face.

In the back of my mind, however, I felt that I'd be happier doing something that made a bit more of a difference in the world.

Aid work was so difficult to get into without at least a Masters degree and I wasn't sure enough to commit three to four years of my life to studying. I'd be twenty-seven by the time I got out, and surely that's far too old to be starting a career.

I was stuck with the question. Should I stop daydreaming about greener pastures and get on with making something of myself in a job that I'm obviously good at? Or do I look for something I believe in?

Then Roadtrip Nation came along, and I got to ask people who had already been there and made these decisions what they thought. I realized that the music industry just wasn't for me—I had nothing in common with the people, and didn't really like the lifestyle. But talking to people who were involved in the charity and aid sector really inspired me—everything they said, I related to.

It was an incredibly powerful feeling, and for the first time in my life I knew what I wanted. I didn't know how I was going to do it, but I knew for sure that what I was going to do with my life was help people in some way.

Since the roadtrip I've been volunteering for charities here in London, enjoying the feeling of somehow making a difference in people's lives, but also narrowing down the field of work that I want to go into.

Before, I looked at people like Nathan Gray—a man that we interviewed in San Francisco who founded Earth Train—and saw them as supermen. But through talking to all the people we met with last summer, I realized that it doesn't work this way—pretty much anyone can be one of these supermen or superwomen, you just have to find that one thing that drives you.

I've found my one thing now, and I'm confident that I can go out there and be all that I want to be, and I've got a shot at being one of those supermen.

Matthew Maude

UK Team

Summer 2005 Roadtrip Reflection

In March 2005, three months before Roadtrip Nation took me across America within six weeks, through some of the most beautiful country this side of heaven, meeting some of the best people born onto this earth, I was working and living in Leeds, UK. A city 250 miles north of London, nestled in the Yorkshire Dales, among the puddings, sheep, and the infamous ale.

Since I was fifteen years old, I'd been working in the film industry. Starting out as a camera trainee, I tried every role from being an actor to an editor, a writer to a director. I'd played the role of Scott Booth in a national soap opera for nine months, acted on the London stage, written for ITV, directed for MTV2, and edited for the BBC. My future lay somewhere within this creative field, but I had no idea as to which particular role I should choose. So I came to the roadtrip wanting to discover more about my ambitions, to figure out how I could be all the things I wanted to be, and how to be amazing at them, too.

But deeper still was the feeling of needing personal growth. Having worked from an early age, I felt like I missed out on a huge amount of self-learning. Coupled with leaving school at seventeen years old to pursue my acting career, and never going to university, I felt like I still needed to learn more about life, myself, and all the other clichés that I had yet to define. With Roadtrip Nation in the summer of 2005, I traveled from New York to Los Angeles, covering 12,000 miles across thirty states with my brother and my best friend—a friend so close, it was a wonder to all that I did not share blood with him.

Over that summer we interviewed thirty people from a diverse set of jobs: the head of NASA, the head of UNICEF, a priest, a trucker. Through these people, their stories, and their histories, we learned more about ourselves than I think we dared to dream of. And we dreamed so much. Although not all our questions about the future were answered, we ended the summer with the ability to ask the questions we needed to find the right answers.

Personally, I also came back with more confidence in my work. And so the trip changed me, it made me look on the world with clearer eyes. It made me look at myself with less doubt and more certainty.

Laura Morris
Canadian Team
Summer 2005 Roadtrip Reflection

My generation is very different from ones in the past. We are media-absorbed, technologically-savvy, and unbelievably affluent by global comparison.

What, if any, are the consequences of this reality?

I believe that one direct result of this exposure and acceptance of media communications is that my generation has a tremendous amount of motivation to search for a career with extrinsic rewards: fame, power, wealth, status. Furthermore, not only do we want these things, but we want them by the time we are twenty. We see examples of people who have achieved this type of success in their twenties and evaluate ourselves by comparison to them.

On the road, I realized that this quest is counterproductive and harmful to many. The goals that twentysomethings have set for themselves are not realistic and, more than likely, are very rarely achieved. Straight out of university, students increasingly have problems engaging the world around them to build the skills that will help them professionally. We want to be on the other side of the river before we even begin to paddle.

Roadtrip Nation has been an inspiration to me, its viewers, and grant recipients by encouraging people to understand the importance of the journey we are taking in life, both professionally and personally. It provides the setting for young people to stop, in potentially one of the richest times in their lives, for new opportunities, and take the time to actualize themselves in a way that university never fostered. And, it does all of this for a generation that desperately needs self-awakening.

Roadtrip Nation has a positive impact on nearly everyone who surrounds the project, not just the viewers and teams I have just mentioned. The individuals I interviewed on the road cherished their opportunity to engage my generation in dynamic discourse and often learned things about themselves during the course of the interviews. Families that simply read the motto on the back of the RV and had never seen the show were excited about the project and hoped that their children might one day participate. At any age and any point of life, the Roadtrip Nation Movement resonates with people, and there is intelligence behind their rallying.

The Movement

More than a book, a documentary, and a Web site, Roadtrip Nation exists to ignite a movement—a movement to help everyone find their own roads by going out, listening to others, and sharing their experiences with the community.

Feed the Movement—and Feed Off It

In this book we shared our experience with you. Now we hope you'll share your experiences with others. Once you've interviewed leaders, don't keep it to yourself. Plug into the movement and share what you learned. The online voice of Roadtrip Nation is our Web site. Visit it: www.roadtripnation.com.

Explore. Plug in. Amplify. Engage.
Join the Movement.

Find the Open Road

Remember the noise? How can you forget it. Everywhere you turn, people tell you who to be and what to do with your life. Block it. Shed it. Leave it for the conformists. As a generation we need to get back to focusing on individuality. Self-construction rather than mass production. That's what finding the open road is all about: connecting your individuality with a path that accentuates it.

How do you find that path? You explore.

Exploring opens your mind.

Exploring opens the world to you, exposing paths that you never knew existed.

Exploring—is how you find the open road.

From the road,
Mike, Nathan, and Brian

FROM THE COAUTHOR

I started writing this book in the same spirit that Mike and Nathan began their roadtrip. After I graduated Indiana University in 1991, I wondered how to turn my love of writing into a career. Instead of jumping into journalism, I took what I thought was a more practical route and spent six years in marketing.

My heart wasn't in it. Every time I talked to a journalist on the phone, I wanted to be doing their job, not mine. Eventually I found the courage to pursue my true passion. I quit my job, went to graduate school for journalism, and then moved to New York, where I've been working as a business journalist since 1997.

About four years later I met Mike and Nathan when they were in New York City to interview people as part of their roadtrip. I wrote a story about them for Forbes, and a few months later we decided to collaborate on this book. They needed a cowriter, and I believed in their mission.

To help record their roadtrip for the book, I watched videotape of every interview that Mike and Nate conducted. I listened intently, transcribed the interviews word for word, and then crafted profiles. We wanted our readers to feel as if they were with Mike and Nate at every interview—whether in the RV or someone's office—listening in on the conversation. We strove to be true to people's voices, to communicate their main messages, and to recreate their inspiring energies.

The profiles in this book appear almost verbatim, although we had to make some changes because people express themselves more colloquially when they speak. We corrected grammar, verb tense, and sentence structure so that each profile would be easy to follow and understand. We rarely changed the words people used, except to clarify a point, but we did change the order in which things were said, as long as the meaning and context remained the same.

Everyone deserves to discover his or her own road, and Mike, Nathan, and I hope <u>Roadtrip Nation</u> will help you find yours. Enjoy the ride.

Joanne Gordon
New York, 2003

from the coauthor

THANK YOU

To think that a few guys in a motorhome built Roadtrip Nation is a huge misperception. The movement was built and <u>belongs</u> to a significant group of individuals who have contributed their energy and spirit to this cause.

Even on our first trip, the amount of people who helped us book the interviews, put us up for the night, point us in the right direction, or fix the RV was extraordinary. When you expose yourself and depend on people around you to that degree, it makes you realize how much good there is in the world. A special thanks to all those who went out of their way to help us get on the road and around the country.

Then, once we came home, a whole new batch of people helped to create a movement out of our trip. Some of them acted as guides, exposing us to the potential and need for the movement—others acted as mentors, equipping us with the skills to turn the idea into a reality—some rolled up their sleeves and worked on it day to day—and others simply believed in it, taking risks that opened up new opportunities. For all those who stepped up and believed in Roadtrip Nation when it was just an idea on a pad of paper—thank you. The movement would not be alive today if it wasn't for you.

Finally, a special thanks to all the people who are making Roadtrip Nation happen today. Those of you who edit the footage, help with bookkeeping, offer new partnership ideas, share RTN on campus, spread the word through the PBS community, and help us to shape the road ahead for Roadtrip Nation—thank you.

In so many ways, Roadtrip Nation is just beginning. Everything that has happened brought us to this point so, together, we can take it to the next level. We're honored that you've chosen Roadtrip Nation to be a part of your open road. Your work is inspiring millions of others to discover their own.

Special thanks to our sponsors and partners:

Corporation
for Public
Broadcasting

thank you

THE FINAL WORD
FROM MIKE, NATHAN, AND BRIAN

A Movement for All Ages

When we first started sharing our roadtrip experience, we thought it would only resonate with other college students. Al the time that was the only age group we understood, because that was who we were.

Three years later, this book and the Roadtrip Nation documentary series on PBS have exposed millions of people to the idea of finding The Open Road.

Truth be told, many of those people have not been college students. They are high school students pressured to pick the right university; twentysomethings waiting tables because they are unsure of what else to do; thirtysomethings looking to change paths to find something they love; or forty and fiftysomethings looking to stay true to their own evolving individuality.

In the last few years we've learned that the Roadtrip Nation idea is not just for college students. It's for anyone trying to define their own road—at any stage of their life. It's not for a certain demographic subset of the population—it's for any openminded individual looking for something more.

Take Alastair Paulin, now managing editor of <u>Mother Jones</u> magazine. It wasn't until his thirties that he and his wife created "our own Roadtrip Nation."

"So I ended up at this investment bank. It was the last place in the world that I should have been, but they offered me more money than I ever imagined I would make. I hated it. You know, I was just faking it. So I quit that job, took the money that they paid me, and my wife and I went backpacking around the world for eighteen months. We sold everything. We gave up our apartment in the city, had one little backpack each, and just hit the road. Neither one of us was doing what we wanted to be doing with our lives—and we hoped that a big part of that trip would be to find a sense of who we really were. Who would we be when we didn't have daily expectations? What choices would we make if we didn't have to be somewhere the next day—when we didn't have to go to a meeting or be on that conference call? We thought that maybe the freedom would help us work out what we really wanted to do with our lives. So in a way, it was our own Roadtrip Nation; we were definitely searching for those answers. Maybe it wasn't a great idea financially, but I would say that it was an investment in ourselves and in our life experience—an investment that would help us figure out what we wanted out of life."

—from the Roadtrip Nation interview with Alastair Paulin,
managing editor of <u>Mother Jones</u> magazine

Alastair's journey dwarfs our three-month roadtrip—but that doesn't make ours any less meaningful. Or yours.

The growth you'll encounter from hitting the road is not time and distance dependent. What matters is where you're at in your life, and how open you are to the experience.

If you can only get one week off from work and don't have much to spend, make the most of it. Pack up your car and head off to a corner of the country you haven't been to yet. Expose yourself to that new world and meet the people within it who are living lives in line with their own individuality. Perhaps they can help you do the same.

Even if you've found your open road, taking a roadtrip to re-calibrate and make sure you're staying true to yourself never hurts. In the last few years, we've found paths we're passionate about—but we still hit the road every summer to gauge ourselves.

We all evolve and change—but how do we recognize and acknowledge that growth if our noses are always at the grind-stone? Hitting the road is simply an exercise in stepping away from life, so you can see it more clearly.

Knowing what you want to do does not have to be something you figure out in your twenties, and then hit cruise control for the rest of your life. You never want to fall asleep at the wheel—life's just too short.

ABOUT THE AUTHORS

Mike Marriner, Nathan Gebhard, and **Brian McAllister** are from California. Nathan and Mike met in sixth grade, and have been friends ever since. Brian and Mike played water polo together in college, and since then the three have embarked on several eye-opening experiences.

Post-college, feeling sheltered and underexposed to the world around them, they hit the road in an unsound 1985 green RV to connect with people who defined their own roads in life. Contrary to what they had learned in school or from growing up in California, they discovered that people can build lives in line with their individuality.

That trip inspired them to create Roadtrip Nation, a grassroots organization that mobilizes students to hit the road and explore the world for themselves. Footage from these trips are shared with people all over, through the Roadtrip Nation Series on PBS, books, various broadcast partnerships, and online at www.road-tripnation.com

Joanne Gordon has been a reporter and writer at <u>Forbes</u> magazine since April 1998 and has written about management, career, and workplace issues for the past ten years. Before becoming a professional writer, Joanne spent six years in marketing and, in 1997, earned a graduate degree from the Medill School of Journalism at Northwestern University. She graduated from Indiana University in 1991 with a B.A. in journalism. Unlike her coauthors, the closest she comes to surfing is rollerblading through Central Park in New York City, where she lives.

find the open road @ www.roadtripnation.com

The Roadtrip Nation Web site is the on-line hub for the movement where you can:
- Get the Roadtrip Nation **Documentary**
- Check out **Video Clips** of the leaders you read about in this book (and a bunch of others that are not in this book)
- **Share** your own experience and read about the experiences of others who have joined the movement.
- Learn how to get the Roadtrip Nation Movement started on **your campus**.

We invite you to come join the movement @ www.roadtripnation.com